CH00536082

OTHER WORLDS

STEWART CONN was born in Glasgow, grew up in Ayrshire and has for many years lived in Edinburgh. Publications include *The Breakfast Room* (2010 Scottish Mortgage Investment Trust Poetry Book of the Year), *Aspects of Edinburgh*, a selected volume *The Touch of Time*, and as editor *100 Favourite Scottish Poems* and *100 Favourite Scottish Love Poems*. A memoir *Distances* and several of his stage plays have also appeared in print. As head of BBC Scotland's radio drama department he championed a wide range of writers. He is a fellow of the RSAMD; was from 2002 to 2005 Edinburgh's inaugural makar; and in 2006 received the Institute for Contemporary Scotland's Iain Crichton Smith award for services to literature.

He has visited and holidayed on many of Scotland's islands, and caught (or failed to catch) trout in many of their lochs and lochans.

OTHER WORLDS

AN ANTHOLOGY OF
SCOTTISH ISLAND POEMS

Edited by
Stewart Conn

Polygon

This paperback first published in Great Britain in 2022
by Polygon, an imprint of Birlinn Ltd.

Birlinn Ltd
West Newington House
10 Newington Road
Edinburgh
EH9 1QS

www.polygonbooks.co.uk

9 8 7 6 5 4 3 2 1

Introduction © Stewart Conn, 2022
Reflections on a Marine Venus by Lawrence Durrell (Faber & Faber, 1953);
The Islands of Scotland by Hugh MacDiarmid (C. Scribner's Sons, 1939)
I Crossed the Minch by Louis MacNeice (Longmans, Green & Co, 1938)
My life and Times: Octave Six 1924–1930
by Compton Mackenzie (Chatto & Windus, 1967)

ISBN 978 1 84697 541 7

All rights reserved. No part of this publication may be reproduced,
stored, or transmitted in any form, or by any means, electronic,
mechanical or photocopying, recording or otherwise, without
the express written permission of the publisher.

British Library Cataloguing-in-Publication Data
A catalogue record for this book is available on request
from the British Library.

Typeset in Verdigris MVB by Polygon, Edinburgh
Printed and bound by CPI Group (UK) Ltd, Croydon CR0 4YY

CONTENTS

III. ISLAND LIFE

IV. LOVE AND LOSS

V. CREATURES

VI. FROM AFAR

INTRODUCTION

In a list of unclassified diseases in a friend's notebook, Lawrence Durrell came across *Islomania*, defined as 'a rare but by no means unknown affliction of the spirit' affecting those who find islands somehow irresistible. For such *islomanes*, he observed, 'the mere knowledge that they are on an island, a little world surrounded by the sea, fills them with an indescribable intoxication'. That this related purely to the Aegean would have had Hugh MacDiarmid fuming: 'I know the Isles of Greece myself: they are not fit to be mentioned in the same breath as the Hebrides'.

Set against Durrell's *Paradise Terrestre* and a yearning for some lost Atlantis could be misty visions of Tír na nÓg, source of everlasting youth and home of mythical Celtic heroes. Hand in hand with this it is claimed that many folk sense their identity, and centrality, most strongly when on the periphery. But others are disposed to head for the island of their choice for more prosaic reasons: as sightseers, out of curiosity, from a sense of adventure, hoping to recharge their batteries or simply to get away from it all.

Scotland's islands – some eight hundred or so, the vast bulk comprising Orkney, Shetland and the Hebrides – are vital, not just to a cartography of the country (imagine our tourist trade without them), but to its disparate culture, history, economy and national identity. Inhabited or deserted, archipelago or solitary rock, boasting skerries or silver strand, peatbog, machair or fertile acres, it is impossible to conceive of a national psyche in which they are not deeply embedded. As unthinkable would be a Scottish literature or poetry without them.

Their imprint is palpable in those who through birthright and inheritance can relay at first hand the realities and heartbeat of island life. But most of us, though mainlanders, have surely been visitors, however briefly. I retain early childhood memories of paddle-steamer trips down the Firth of Clyde, the band playing and a red sun sinking behind Arran's 'sleeping warrior'. On a first trip to Skye my wife and I, fleeing Sligachan's non-stop downpour and midges, encountered a shift in the weather and spent a glorious week at Elgol. Later would come family holidays on South Uist and South Harris; visits to the St Magnus Festival and other stays in Orkney; unforgettable glimpses of Iona, Canna and Islay; and under a steely east-coat light, boat-trips to the Bass Rock, Inchcolm and the Isle of May.

Many of my poems have island settings. But for this volume it was those by other folk which set my pulse racing, through a sharpening of memory or in opening new vistas and evoking new worlds and states of mind, from Barra and Eriskay to Luing, Mingulay and the Isle of May; Inchcape and the Torran rocks to Taransay and Tiree. Varying in length, form, music and intensity, some of these alternatively capture an almost abstract beauty or bleakness while others, including many depicting island life and relationships, touch the heart-strings. Cumulatively they proved, and will I hope here provide, a captivating hunting-ground.

I sought initially a core of established poets themselves island born and/or bred, spanning native Gaelic-speakers Derick Thomson and Angus Peter Campbell, Orcadian George Mackay Brown, and Christine De Luca and Robert Alan Jamieson, their mother tongue Shetlandic. Then came others who, rather than necessarily belonging to this island or that, write richly and diversely *about* them. At this stage I became particularly conscious of Louis MacNeice's reminder in *I Crossed the Minch* that however 'tantalised by the islands and seduced by them' the poetical tripper may become, 'on that soil he will always be an outsider'. But I saw no reason why even the most fleeting visitor, whether looking in or out and besides offering a fresh scenic perspective, shouldn't be capable of bottling something of an island's essence.

Of longer poems which have given me lasting pleasure I forewent Douglas Dunn's 'St Kilda's Parliament' and 'Hallaig' by Sorley Maclean, both readily accessible elsewhere, and preferring the latter's 'Am Bàta Dubh/The Black Boat', its clear-cut central image crystallising Greek and Gaelic sea pursuits. Edwin Muir's 'The Horses' and Ruthven Todd's 'In September 1937' I also regretfully excluded, to rule out any overlap with Alexander McCall Smith's anthology *A Gathering* which this volume could be seen as complementing, especially through the exciting new generation represented here by South Uist born Niall Campbell, Miriam Nash who was raised on Erraid, Shetlander Roseanne Watt and others hitherto new to me who have similarly won their spurs.

Rich depictions of island flora and fauna sit alongside sightings of croft dwellers and ferry-lowpers. Expressions of affection and accounts of imprisonment and bereavement sit cheek-by-jowl with evocations of drowned sailors, corporeal and ghostly. Praise poems alternate with diary entries and holiday postcards. Others cover stretches of water: Corryvreckan, say, or the Minch. And while there is a recurring sense of island heritage, and of belonging, the poet's feet need not be actively on island soil or on the deck of a fishing-boat: Helen B. Cruickshank's yearning is sparked by a glimpse of someone wearing a Harris tweed jacket, in London's very different Strand; while for Hamish Whyte, back home again, a family photo triggers a sharp tang of memory.

An island can be a source of escape or return, of solace or threat. Folk-memory, and a sense of exile or loss, can be quickened in a variety of ways: Laurna Robertson's 'Photocall: Lerwick 1898' lists a group of her forebears, many to be dispersed about the globe; Stewart Sanderson's 'On Eriskay' was triggered by a documentary by a German ethnographer. Of the book's linguistic variants the twin versions of Harry Josephine Giles's 'Visa Wedding' declare not just their place of origin but a deep-seated dual identity. And outsider attitudes vary from that of Nikki Robson squelching to the tourist office in 'The Callanish Stones' to those, like Alan Riach's on Tiree, 'there to be seen and noted,/on the human side of the vanishing point' ('Vanishing Point').

From the hoard of traditional material accessible I've added a small spicing of personal favourites: a fragment ascribed to Saint Columba, a twelfth-century paean for 'Arran of the many stags' and an extract from an Icelandic saga recording a raid on the Western Isles; and further worlds (and centuries) apart, 'The Great Silkie of Sule Skerry' and an account of a nineteenth-century Duke of Hamilton barring his Arran estate to orphans from the mainland, which strikes a sadly topical note. Beyond these, which I like to think fit in seamlessly, I steered clear of the many popular songs and shanties which, however exhilarating, I felt would either not pull their weight poetically, or seem simply out of place.

I trust that *Other Worlds* will evoke something of the islands both in their totality and in their breath-taking diversity. Dominant naturally are the inter-dependent realms of land and water, many of whose denizens are locked in their element but others, like the closely observed seals in Samuel Tongue's 'Hauling Out', balanced on boulders and able to 'rock gently on the point between two worlds.' In tune, too, with the anthology's title are Jackie Kay's 'I always looked out at the world/And wondered if the world looked back at me' ('Yell Sound') and the vivid ending to Alison Flett's 'Harbour': 'taygether we watched/thi big ball o sun/slip slowly/smoothly/over thi ej/o oor wurld/and inty/anuther.'

Sir Compton Mackenzie, on purchasing the Shiants in the Outer Hebrides, observed: 'To most people [they] mean nothing. To some they mean the most acute bout of sea-sickness between Kyle and Stornoway as the MacBrayne steamer wallows in the fierce overfalls that guard them. To a very few they mean a wild corner of fairyland, the memory of which remains for ever in the minds of those who have visited their spellbound cliffs and caves'.

However high-flown, even idyllic, his summation is not necessarily so far-fetched. Long or short, an island sojourn may release a pent-up emotional charge, serve as an act of pilgrimage or provide a source of healing and replenishment. Nor is it rare for a literal island to conjure up another in the imagination; even make it appear, as for Andrew Greig on Cava, 'as though one were moving through/not an island/but a poem of an island,/as in a way one is . . .' ('Shelter').

In *The Islands of Scotland*, MacDiarmid wrote: 'One goes (or should go) to an island for happiness, not pleasure' – the title of his short poem here chiming with his claim that 'the proper main object of recourse to islands . . . is, or ought to be, perfection'. It is my hope that, in evoking them, the poems in this selection will not only give pleasure, and recall moments of happiness, but enable the Scottish Islands, all the more magically, to exert their spell.

Stewart Conn

RESOLVE

All I know is, there must come
times more wondrous which will
set white horses dancing, in our
nostrils the fragrance of far islands.

Stewart Conn
from *The Touch of Time*, Bloodaxe

I. CROSSINGS

IONA FERRY

It's the smell I remember –
The dizziness of diesel, tarry rope, wood sheened
   like toffee.
The sea was waving in the wind, a dancing –
I wanted it to be rough and yet I didn't.
My mother and I snugged under the awning,
To a dark rocking. We were as low as the waves,
All of us packed in tight like bales of wool.

The engine roared alive, its tremor
Juddered through the wood and thrilled me, beat
   my heart.
The shore began fading behind the white curl of our
   hum.
Fourteen days lay barefoot on the island –
Still asleep, their eyes all shut.
And yet I knew them all already,
Felt them in my pocket like polished stones –
Their orchids, their hurt-white sand, their larksong.

Kenneth Steven

ARRIVAL OF THE FERRY AT LOCHMADDY

It's still miles out in the Minch
but much closer than a dot on the horizon

and you won't see me   but I wave anyway

as you pass the Madadhs
a group on the outside deck looks like you
and I begin our wave
both arms in a sort of half star jump
without the jump   but jumping as well from time to time

and I'm not looking round
not caring who's looking at me   I'm focussed
focussed on the small group   but they don't wave back

then I catch my first sight
two big   two much smaller   higher up
than where I was looking   all doing our star jump wave

                              at the end of the pier
I'm as close as I can get without falling into the sea
still waving   now yelling   and you're yelling back

berthing the boat takes   forever
before they hoist the steps up to the door
I'm waiting at the bottom

you are first off the boat

                    Pauline Prior-Pitt

The Madadhs are two rocks at the entrance to Lochmaddy bay.

BETWEEN THE TERMINALS

And the ferryman stopped her,
hand raised, when her car edged out too soon
from the rest and rolled onto the linkspan.
Uneasy, we wait as waves hush on cold stones.

In half-light on the shore below
a strand silvers, a silk shift left
heavy and wet on the rocks.
Full-bodied and soft a seal lies still.

The ferryman's dues are paid. The ramp
is lowered; light floods from the deck.
Her car leads on, bright with flowers,
and stands at the prow alone.

Loaded, the boat sways round the Holm
into the Flow. Circling islands bob by
broken roofs breasting the sky.
The wash, unfurling, laps at empty nousts.

Like stars the Mainland lights
glint at the stern. Dawn kindles the horizon.
Wintering seabirds lift from the waves
and flicker, rafting on air.

At Lyness, the watchers gather
beyond the looming gantry. Sea urchins
stud the breakwater, womb-like pods
a glimmer of pink below the tilting surface.

She goes out, flower-laden,
under the bow into the day's brilliance.

                              Yvonne Gray

SUNDAY ON THE LUING SOUND

All day the sailboats have been langorous in their gliding
  between Belnahua
      its quarry denuded deep water
      nursing cuttings anchoring this ring of island
         and its roofless slate cottages
      to seawater, one mile offshore
and the Fladda Lighthouse
      its walled garden
         sheltering brambles the common twayblade
      two keepers' cottages standing empty a colony
         of terns chattering at closed doors
      the tall white masthead
         a watchtower reporting No Danger

White sails blow taut like the corners
  of hospital sheets   each gust a snap
         a reminder to be grateful
the sun bleaching blue water and blue air   into white

Then
  the fisherman's seiner speeds past engine gunning
         a running mackerel   dark greens of work above
         its irridescent belly barnacled   below the surface
            hand-tied buoys flailing in wind
               like a fistful of carnival balloons
         its silver hull flashes through froth
         hugs the shoreline heads for home

                Marjorie Lotfi

AM BÀTA DUBH

A bhàta dhuibh, a Ghreugaich choimhlionta,
cluas siùil balg siùil làn is geal,
agus tu fhéin gu foirfeach ealanta,
sàsmhach uallach gun ghiamh gun ghais;
do chùrsa réidh gun bhròn gun fhaireachadh;
cha b'iadsan luingis dhubha b'ealanta
a sheòl Odysseus a nall á Itaca
no Mac Mhic Ailean a nall á Uidhist,
cuid air muir fion-dhorcha
's cuid air sàl uaine-ghlas.

Somhairle MacGill-Eain

THE BLACK BOAT

Black boat, perfect Greek,
sail tack, sail belly full and white,
and you yourself complete in craft,
silent, spirited, flawless;
your course smooth, sorrowless, unfeeling;
there were no more skilled black ships
that Odysseus sailed over from Ithaca
or Clanranald over from Uist,
those on a wine-dark sea,
those on a grey-green brine.

Sorley MacLean

THE ARRAN SMACKS

Shon McPhail was an Arran man,
   And a mariner bold was he;
He owned a smack called the *Betsy Ann*,
   Which he sailed through the briny sea.

He lifted his sand in Lamlash Bay,
   And rockery stones as well;
Then for Glasgow city he sailed away,
   The stones and his sand to sell.

Tatties and scones, some bread and kail
   Were the stores that he had on board;
For the times were bad, and Shon McPhail
   Could no better than these afford.

'Heigh, ho!' he says, 'it's gey hard on me
   That, after a fortnight's run,
I maun sell my sand on the Glesca Quay
   At five or six bob a ton.

Then load up coals for hame again
   At a most ridiculous freight,
And their reason for this, they tell me plain,
   Is because I'm no' up-to-date.'

The puffers, he says, have killed his trade,
  And the days of the smacks have gone;
And there isn't a living now to be made
  For the likes of poor old Shon.

Though things for him look mighty black,
  Still it never can be denied,
It was men like him and his Arran smack
  That helped to make the Clyde.

                    Paddy Coffey

FISHING FROM THE BACK OF ROUSAY

Iceland, they say, is nearest. There, the waves
Originate, and roll – like rolling graves –
Towards these umber cliffs. Green seaweed paves

Like sloppy ice (but slippier) the stairs
Of rock you must descend. Then what impairs
Your fall down fifteen flights to lobster-lairs

Is only, now and then, a limpet's hand
So small and rough, and clenched. And where you stand
When you have reached the foot, is not dry land.

For one by one the rollers rise and swell
And swell some more, and swell: you cannot tell
If this will fall (Boom) where the last one fell

Or (Crash) on your own head. But, bait your hook
 And cast in a deep channel; while you look
You're left to fish in a salt-water brook

That fills till it's Atlantic. Fine, you sigh,
A bite at any minute. Where's the sky?
Boom, Boom, it says, you're drowned! – Then it's rolled by.

                              Ian Hamilton Finlay

NOVEMBER FROM THE CLACH RATHAD

The Canna lighthouse, smearing out the sky
of soft grey halfway indigo,
talks to Tex Geddes on the coast of Rum,
his masthead light now making steady north
for Soay harbour on a full flood tide:
a car – just headlamps on a hill –
plunges from skyline down to Tarskavaig,
and a daft dog in Drinan barks
at the sudden shadow of a black cow's bulk;
a blackbird stutters and a snipe
startles along the shadowed ditch. It is the time
when searches are abandoned,
when the doe rabbit I stunned against a stone
shivers suddenly long past her death;
and the tilted landscape,
like a capsized sail, dips into the sea
of northern latitude so deep in indigo
it seems we'll never right ourselves
before Orion swings into the dark
certain to hunt us down.

John Purser

I'LL BOIL THE KETTLE

I'll boil the kettle since the mainlight's on
breaking areas of angle-poise arcs
on colour-coded panels of contacts.

The skipper of the *Golden Sheaf* can
pass the tow by radio-telephone:
'Over to you, Calum, at Loch Sealg.
The bacon and eggs are on, below
and I'd better see about getting a crust
to share between the boys on Friday.'

That tone is set against the residue
of another task, a further latitude,
clear of the Butt and at eight degrees west
A crewman simply went over the rails.
He jumped out to the calm night.
They threw fluorescence, lowered a boat.

We sent a chopper with potent spans
of live fights. It found only
lit buoys and flotation as
a brash litany of failed hopes.

Ian Stephen

BY FERRY TO THE ISLAND

We crossed by ferry to the bare island
where sheep and cows stared coldly through the wind –
the sea behind us with its silver water,
the silent ferryman standing in the stern
clutching his coat about him like old iron.

We landed from the ferry and went inland
past a small church down to the winding shore
where a white seagull fallen from the failing
chill and ancient daylight lay so pure
and softly breasted that it made more dear

the lesser white around us. There we sat,
sheltered by a rock beside the sea.
Someone made coffee, someone played the fool
in a high rising voice for two hours.
The sea's language was more grave and harsh.

And one sat there whose dress was white and cool.
The fool sparkled his wit that she might hear
new diamonds turning on her naked finger.
What might the sea think or the dull sheep
lifting its head through heavy Sunday sleep?

And later, going home, a moon rising
at the end of a cart-track, minimum of red,
the wind being dark, imperfect cows staring
out of their half-intelligence, and a plough
lying on its side in the cold, raw

naked twilight, there began to move
slowly, like heavy water, in the heart
the image of the gull and of that dress,
both being white and out of the darkness rising
the moon ahead of us with its rusty ring.

Iain Crichton Smith

THE WAR

When call-up papers came
he rode his finest gelding
to Lochboisdale Ferry,
a cartwheel broken
in the shed, eggs uncollected,
jobs on the croft unfinished,
his favourite collie mewling
on its chain. He left
with other crofting lads,
Neil Johnstone from Eochar
Angus Mackay the piper
Ian Conelly from Borinish.
Hooves deep in campion and furze,
the bent-grass racing wind,
a sky-lark's requiem high
in the boiling cloud-mass.

He felt the ferry loll and list,
the silver shoreline dip and rise,
until his palm could hide
the granite ramparts of the quay
the crouching crofts,
the cattle small as flies.
Rolling a cigarette against the rail
he saw the machair disappear
then reappear in wraiths of haar,
and disappear for aye
behind a knuckled fist of sea,
his agitated steed calmed

with round vowels of home
until the ferry, bucking
on the wayward tide
was tethered safe on Kyle.

Chrys Salt
from *Weaver of Grass*

LONE SEAL TRAVELLING SOUTH

It was the kind of night when midges flitted
all ways in the windless night air
their wings transparent in golden sunlight
and sparrows whirred softly past
as you sat at your front door,
a lazy quietness taking hold of the place
and the village at peace with itself.
On such a night I took myself off to the shore
to catch another luminous sunset over Mull
and as I sat overlooking the calmest of calm bays
a lone seal came following the coast at dusk
travelling south along the Luing shore
every so often leaping out of the water
ducking down and with a flip disappearing
deep into that world of fish and clams
and all that seals dream of
to emerge further south along the coast
moving ever closer to the Ponds
where the big seals hole up on Glas Eilean,
and it was then I took to thinking
of that playful journey home
that we all make alone in the end
wandering the coast leaving no trace
but the lapping of waves on shore.

Norman Bissell

VISITING ARRAN WITH MY MOTHER

The year you died, we kidnapped you,
stole the wheelchair, tanks of oxygen,
and, of course, the morphine.

Sorry sorry sorry, you said as we hauled you
up the ferry steps, your legs buckling, refusing
to bear your weight, those same legs which
aged seven or eight, had soared you
to the summit of Goat Fell, your father
hirpling, out of breath, behind.

The following day we waited for dark clouds to pass,
tucked you under tartan rugs, took you to your
great-grandfather, wheelchair rutting the sodden grass.
On a slope above the bay, by his weathered stone
we lost you to a whispered conversation
only the spirits and the Holy Isle could hear.

On Lamlash beach, grinning and with giddy glee,
you teetered from the chair, stooped and scooped
a fit of silver sand, let it trickle through your hand.
Later, you said you'd heard, soft, insistent as the waves,
your sisters chattering as they played by the water's edge.
Your little sisters long since dead.

On the ferry as we left, you gazed at memories fading
to the past, when from the waves a sudden dolphin leapt
– another and another and another – sleek creatures
curving high, slicing down beneath the swell,
bidding you a final, an exuberant farewell.

Magi Gibson

HARBOUR

Ah kent yi wir cummin
an goin
thi ebb an flo
o ma
body clenchin
letting go
clenchin
letting go
lets go
down tay the harbour
ah sayz tay ma lassy
ma first born
see thi boats cummin in

an we stood taygither
at the endy the peer
lookn outwards
trine tay mind oan
thi namesy thi boats

cum hame boy gordon
we called oot
cum hame girl mina
john L

cum hame two belles
storm drift
silver wave

cum hame sunrise
radiant queen
an they came

rite inuff
thi way they do
thin tiny black specs o thum
pulsin larger
taywords us

over wotter
sun frostid
rippuld
rinkuld
lie bathroom glass
hidin deep
domestic secrets

ma body clenched
again
deepur
and ah reeched doon
tay clasp
thi smilin hand
o ma first one

taygether we watched
thi big ball o sun slip slowly
smoothly
over thi ej
o oor world
and inty
anuther.

Alison Flett

II. LOCH AND MOOR

FROM BEINN ASLAIG

The dog bounds over the moorland,
bright with tormentil, bedstraw, milkwort,
yellow, white and blue, magenta orchids,
butterwort nodding, cotton-grass streaming.
Lark and pippet song bubbles through the air,
lochans gaze straight into heaven,
their blue blotted from the sea far below.
I see the roads I take every day
over grey-green Sleat, lochan-lit,
look over Glenelg and horned Beinn Sgritheall,
to Loch Hourn and Loch Nevis carving up the coast,
to the folding Cuillins folded into cloud.

What has this over any other place
of peak and moorland, sea and shoreline?
Only that I know it, by foot and car and name,
have seen it from every side, in all its moods – and mine,
my eye sweeping flank and groin and shoulder,
lingering like a hand on every mound and hollow.

Meg Bateman

ISLAY LOCH

There was nothing that would attract water
on that flat expanse of moor, nowhere
for rain to run, for streams to flow or gather,
and yet the improbable loch was really there.

It shone with an opaquely amber glint
a little way across the level moor;
I set out on a faint sheep track that went
through feather grass and heather to the shore.

There was no track. There were no other sheep.
And all the earth's irregularities
opened and closed around my stumbling feet;
around my head hung a cloud of horseflies.

From time to time the loch was out of sight
before I reached the edge eventually;
I saw the shifting sediment of peat
make water look like whisky or pale tea.

Appearance and reality appear
to be like interchangeable extremes
when smooth turns rough and the opaque grows clear.
Across an actual moor where far is near
an amber and unlikely loch still gleams.

James Aitchison

FRISK WAATIR TROOT

Afoar he lærns t'sykil a byk
he's tentilie rowin daflatboddim
roond an aroond Melbie logh.

Siks jieir aald
an dark pætie waatir's
slappin at da syd.

He's wurriet'at sumien myght kick
fæ da quhyt-waasht hoos
akross da girssie odoo an sie

waatir siepen in aboot
his rubbir bøt fiet –
an he'd gjit a lugfoo

quahan he wan hem, for no
tellin oniebodie
he lækit denchir to.

Robert Alan Jamieson

> Before he learns to ride a bike, he's carefully rowing the skiff,
>> round and around Melby loch.
> Six years old, and dark peaty water's slapping at the side.
> He's worried that someone might look from the white-washed
>> house across the grassy meadow and see
> Water seeping in about his rubber-boot feet – and he'd get an earful
> When he got home, for not telling, anybody that he likes danger too.

ISLE OF ARRAN

Where no one was was where my world was stilled
into hills that hung behind the lasting water,
a quiet quilt of heather where bees slept,
and a single slow bird in circles winding
round the axis of my head.

Any wind being only my breath, the weather
stopped, and a woollen cloud smothered the sun.
Rust and a mist hung over the clock of the day.
A mountain dreamed in the light of the dark
and marsh mallows were yellow for ever.

Still as a fish in the secret loch alone
I was held in the water where my feet found ground
and the air where my head ended,
all thought a prisoner of the still sense –
till a butterfly drunkenly began the world.

Alastair Reid

AN DÀRNA EILEAN

Nuair a ràinig sinn an t-eilean
bha feasgar ann
's bha sinn aig fois,
a' ghrian a' dol a laighe
fo huibhrig cuain
's am bruadar a' tòiseachadh ás ùr.

Ach anns a' mhadainn
shad sinn dhinn a' chuibhrig
's anns an t-solus gheal sin
chunnaic sinn loch anns an eilean
is eilean anns an loch,
is chunnaic sinn
gun do theich am bruadar pìos eile bhuainn.

Tha an staran cugallach
chon an dàrna eilein,
tha a' chlach air uideil
tha a' dion nan dearcag,
tha chraobh chaorainn a' crlonadh,
fàileadh na h-iadhshlait a' faileachdainn oirnn a-nis.

Ruaraidh MacThòmais

THE SECOND ISLAND

When we reached the island
it was evening
and we were at peace,
the sun lying down
under the sea's quilt
and the dream beginning anew.

But in the morning
we tossed the cover aside
and in that white light
saw a loch in the island,
and an island in the loch,
and we recognised
that the dream had moved away from us again.

The stepping-stones are chancy
to the second island,
the stone totters
that guards the berries,
the rowan withers,
we have lost now the scent of the honeysuckle.

Derick Thomson

BLAEBERRIES!

I cry out, as if I've never seen them before
growing wild on this island. I pinch one

between finger and thumb; velvet
rubs away to reveal its colour.

Her voice comes in pieces through the trees
from the beach – *don't eat that!*

The men have been going back there to –
I let it fall from my hand, small blue-beryl

rabbit dropping. Later, searching
for pine cones up on the island's temples,

out of sight, I find they are everywhere,
dizziness spots, pea-sized, dust-blue

looking cheeky in the undergrowth –
here, where only I have come,

where surely no one ever came
to go. I gather a palmful, burst them

between my teeth: the neat pop
of skin, the grit of seeds, the sweetness

of small islands. Dad calls us
back to the boat, those fish are out there

somewhere. I take three bracken-bound steps,
stop, feel a sudden need

arrive like a tang in the throat, rise up
like a small boy's thumb to his nose.

Angela Cleland

56.1833° N, 2.5667° W

May Island, born under the firth's unstable bed,
an eruption deep within the ritual subconscious.
Sill of an underworld planed by glaciers
crawling east-northeast. Ragged incursions,
occlusions, perspectival falsehoods
wreck boats. Heavily birded, sealed, befouled
and anointed. Its resting heart rate is very low.

'The Isle of May', imposed upon it
by foreigners from the English Ordnance Survey,
represents it on contemporary maps and charts
though not in the hearts of people with any sense.
Virtue has deserted its brackish wells.
Sanctuary, a grave peril, sunk to its neck.
Small freshwater loch like a light left on.

Karen Solie

CRAIGLIATH

island of many inlets
shape bitten by tides
little bays in which to linger
spray reaching to its shoulder

a few strides east to west
out of kilter south to north
island of peaks and corries
remote, bright, various

its obscurity lifting into clarity
a lonely place to be alone
sunbeams sharpened on its ridges
acid water in rock pools

it is a place apart, grey
a thin wedge in blue
where you were abandoned
by an impulse or a tide

island persisting in itself
drawing the mist about it
firm ground to stand on
in a tilting sea and sky.

With hills implied behind cloud
soil impoverished by rain
a few sheep pull at a thin
crop of sedge and drawmoss

island exposed and sheltered
fertile of colours and forms
contained place in which to be
both accurate and expansive

ruined dwellings on open moors
wild goat paths through heather
paths with nowhere to go
where there is nothing to do.

among the sedimentary deposits
intrusions of coarse-grained granite
with crystals of amethyst, topaz
blue-beryl, smoky quartz.

Having rare flowers in profusion
by burns, in flushes, on red rocks
strewn across meadows, solitary
in crevices, on ridges and crags.

With remnants of woodland
birch, rowan and aspen
huddled in ravines
gullies of tern and bracken

a quiet to drive out sense
a wind to lean against
a wind that can drop
to make you doubt your shape.

To the east bare and tranquil
shifting dunes to the west
some couch grass to stabilise
peat sweetened with blown sand

sandpiper piping from a stone
lifting and settling on a stone
far cry of a curlew
a corncrake clearing its throat

the hours long and inconsequential
waving plumes of marram grass
the days harsh and tender
primroses in a nest of rock

where strict limits engage
particulars, set at a distance
from distraction and noise
balanced on the crest of a wave

                        Thomas A. Clark

SCORED WITH A MOON

(Knowe of Skea, Westray)

A house on the shore to lodge what is dumb:
a her or a him fills this vessel of stone.

We mortared the roof, planed the way in,
welcomed no-eye, no-hoof, no-skin.

We leave and return. Our words scuffle the air.
What's within remains calm or not there.

Here is a bird scratched on a bone,
a comb scored with a moon, a stick for a loom.

The tide drags the sea up, then down.
Nothing is uttered or born.

                              Lydia Harris

SHELL BEACH, EIGG

There is no sadness
in it. Shell shingle –

the crunch and crackle
under your boots

in the swash of tides,
a billion husks becoming

sand. And what I love
is the multifarious

abundance,
the sifting shift

in the sea's
dance

of these
miniature sculptures, this

cast up, ruined
city of the salty empires, such

sorted randomness
of patterned time. Look –

that it will never
recur as now

is hardly a thought
for grief. Festival

of the brilliant changes,
a vivid cemetery

where no one mourns
for the shining massacre

of every tide.

                    Gerry Cambridge

SHELTER

Shingle then bedrock then up onto turf.
Our deserted repeat deserted island
– I mean it was abandoned twice –
exhales heather and salt in last light.

Mark makes the *Whaler* fast, thinking
certain announcements shake us to the keel:
overdose; landfall; with child. Checks painter
runs unsnarled through fairlead. Detail,
glory of micro-adventure!

Spray-damp breeks cling and grip, as
tent under one arm, sleeping bags
squashed in oxters, hump-backed under
food and drink, I stumble downwind
seeking shelter before dark –
            a rusty blade
      scraped back to its element,
grey-gleaming, whetted, of use again.

  Coarse grass, tufts and hollows,
  swells, peaks – but not moving.
        I move.
  That 's the difference
  between sailing and walking.

Sheep scatter, terns peep and flash, curlews
follow their own lament downwind.

It is the hour of flecks and blurs.
Quest for *the right place*
   is urgent, tripping, sequential,
   as though one were moving through
not an island
but a poem of an island,
as in a way one is ...

   Are you gonna get that tent up?

Land dips and offers
shelter in lee of static wave.
Drop gear, hurry back, meet Mark
leaving *Whaler* grounded off high water,
   lurched over for the night
as falling asleep we leave the body
lying on its side.

                              Andrew Greig

HYDRA
for D & S & F & A & L

Were we like a plough, ancient or modern,
or a plough like us – as you taught us to *dell*,

to dig as digging used to be done
the four of us side by side, and moving as one

along each new row and down the fallowed yard?
Straining to turn the chunked soil,

we intermittently fell into a genius rhythm:
trod the spade-heads, and teetered while you cut

the corner of the clod; raising our blades
in the fissure to turn the dead weight

of it together and then striking
the same, rolled clod in unison

with spades honed to a thin, ragged edge,
as cobras with their hoods spread dash

from the same knot of muscle.
Just as often I whacked one

of you with my hip or arse or our hat-brims clashed
or the spade just missed the hand that darted

into turned earth for docken root or shards of him
or we eyed Foula, distant

[44]

in blue haze, and panted, or hosed the pig,
who shuddered the water from her curling bristles

and tacked about her park. We filled our hats
at the tap and worked on with earlobes dripping,

while the dryness washed down from our first row,
the turned roots parching in the sun,

until it was done,
in the cooling of the light.

Jen Hadfield

III. ISLAND LIFE

EARLY BUS

Headlights breast the hill,
too far off for any sound
except the tide's wash
slapping the sea wall.

The indicator winks,
engine chuntering,
windows steamed up,
a fug of talk inside
like a travelling pub.
Up two steps, pass ready.

Harbour, love?

Yes, please.

Doors have hissed shut.
The insect bus
creeps on towards Brodick, while outside
dawn tears the black sky open
like a tangerine.

Alison Prince

VANISHING POINT

And here in far Tiree, the scattered houses smiling at each other,
we drive along the roads, recirculating, letting acquaintance deepen.
The white school bus swings over the road on the curving horizon
  behind us,
looms up into our mirrors. And so, with slowing courtesy,
we pull into the passing place and wait for him to overtake
with a modest, friendly wave for acknowledgement.
And the bus drives on, over the gentle curves ahead of us.
Mid-afternoon and this school day has ended.

The houses in their isolated places have fewer, smaller windows
than you might think. They all look out at distances in air and
  land
to sea. Three fields further on, and the road slows down again,
the school bus coming back. Over on the far left field,
a tall young boy swings a satchel from its straps across his shoulder,
skylined as he strides uphill to home, and spares us only a glance.
There are two figures up at the house, and washing on the line.

The breeze picks up and brushes out the hair
of two girls walking towards us by the roadside,
and up on a platform of scaffolding, two men in blue dungaree
  overalls
are working on a roof, repairing beams. I lift my hand and one
  waves
back with a smile, his hand and his mouth scarcely moving.
A minimal act, but there to be seen and noted,
on the human side of the vanishing point.

Alan Riach

AT BARRA AIRPORT

We've wandered all morning on the runway,
dabbling in seawater for shells,
looking out to Eriskay
and the blue Uists.

Reaching the airport, we go in for coffee,
windswept, sand on our shoes.
The phone rings but no one answers it.
All the chairs are turned towards the view.

Out again, with the ocean
humming in our ears,
we sit down to picnic on the dunes
and up snuggles the airport cat.

People begin to gather: porters,
the post bus, an ambulance,
a man with cameras.
Everyone eyes the horizon.

And here it comes now, out of the clouds,
dipping over water, skimming with white wings.
Fragile as a dragonfly,
it lands, on tiptoe, on the cocklestrand.

A bustle of luggage and hugging.
News arriving: letters and papers.
Trucks scrawling tyremarks on the sand,
the cat hissing at a sheepdog.

The air hostess struggles with high heels
and the wind flapping at her kilt.
The pilot stops for a moment,
bends down, picks up a shell.

Elizabeth Burns

EATING ORKNEY

Gone the salt-washed oyster-shell
of sky, the pickieternos' aerobatic jazz,
bass riff of tractor and ferry.
Gone the chorusline of jiving
thrift, the tide's cool blues,
the intemperate applause of gulls.
Gone the indigo intermezzi,
morning's glimmer keeking
between midnight's eyelids.

From a *Dark Island Beer* box,
partans to clean, for tea. I crack
claws, scoop meat, dispose
of still warm dead-man's fingers,
cut my thumb, lick at the sting
of split skin, backtrack to a boat,
the *Northern Lights*, in trouble:
from the dark deep its crew
conjuring Harpy, Siren, Valkyr.

                              Dilys Rose

AN TIGH SEINNSE
a pub in Portnahaven

My hot chocolate comes with its provenance.
The dark-haired waitress
describes how they bring the quality African cocoa
into the island – she leans in, points,
see how the brown is almost purple?
Oh yes, the way the best things always edge towards
being something else.

How small this room is and how
dark the interior,
the still, dry air coiled and threaded
through rafters, like sails
and the furniture that little bit
too close together.

She asks
Have you ever seen a cocoa pod?
I have, I have.
It's this size, like a draw-purse or wee coracle.
You could go to sea in it.
I did, I went to sea in it.
And here I am.

Lynn Davidson

AN T-SEANN CHAIRT AGAINN

Ghiùlain i mìle mìorbhail –
pocan-mòna nach tèid àireamh,
clòimhtean chaorach bhon an àirigh,
badan feòir is cocan-eòrna,

còig gille deug air am pronnadh
agus aon latha foghair
rùda mòr a chaidh a rùsgadh
is faoileag a' danns air adhairc.

Bha an t-each sean is caol ge-tà
's chaidh a reic ri ceàrd bha siubhal,
's ghabh fuaim am Massey Ferguson àit'
gliog is brag na cuibhill.

A' chairt
na fealla-dhà làn-ùine. Air bòrd, sheòl
sinn gu San Francisco, 's dh'èirich pàirt
dhan ghealaich, 's a' chluasag-bheòil

bhiodh ceangal an asail 's na cuibhl'
fhathast nam postan-coise
a' meirgeadh thall an Uibhist.

Aonghas Phàdraig Caimbeul

OUR OLD CART

She bore wonders –
endless sacks of dusty peat,
countless bags of oily wool,
stooks of hay and jagged corn,

fifteen squashed boys,
and one spectacular day
a sheared ram with a stray
gull dancing on its horns.

But the horse grew old
and was sold to a passing tinker,
so the brand-new Massey Ferguson
replaced the bridle's chinkle.

      The cart
became our plaything. It sailed
to San Francisco, and part of it flew
to the moon, and that bit

which connects the axle to the wheel
became a pair of goal-posts which still stand
rusting in the relentless Uist wind.

         Angus Peter Campbell

WITHOUT TREES ON SHETLAND

Only an artist
uncertain of his lines
would add trees to this landscape –
such finery and frippery,
distracting the eye
from the true shape of things.

Here, where they've been rubbed out,
everything's clear.
A clean sweep, no frills,
no nonsense. No trees

and no doubt at all
your Maker
can get a better view of you.

Diana Hendry

LEWISIAN NIGHTS

Abandoned air force buildings – mess hall,
dormitories, clifftop cells where visions
of war were drawn from a metal sea –

have become a village, concrete shells
that sheep wander like tinkers. In the cold war
of wind and land, two crofts remain,

and pillboxes black with peat
guard a beach whose sand
was sucked into the sea.

Cows stand in the rain. Inside, we drink
and talk of ferry crossings, first impressions,
sitting in a crofthouse kitchen

built for radar operators' wives.
At each pause in conversation
we contemplate the inner exile.

Later, our hostess lifts a gun
and none of us is shocked or laughs
as feathers fall near the cattle trough:

the gull flies west with the sun, lead-poisoned.
Night sweeps its ash into the sky.
A bus rattles at the end of the road.

Garry MacKenzie

WRECK

The hulk stranded in Scalpay bay,
Hung like a hall with seaweed, stuck
Its long snout through my holiday.
It lay foundered on its own bad luck.

Twice every day it took aboard
A cargo of the tide; its crew
Flitted with fins. And sand explored
Whatever cranny it came to.

It should have carried deaths to give
To me stumbling across the stones;
It never spoke of what could live.
I saw no ghost between its bones.

It had not learned that it had failed;
Its voyages would not let it be.
More slow than glacier it sailed
Into the bottom of the sea.

Norman MacCaig

THE GAELIC LONG TUNES

On Sabbath days, on circuit days,
the Free Church assembled from boats and gigs
and between sermons they would tauten
and, exercising all they allowed of art,
haul on the long lines of the Psalms.

The seated precentor, touching text,
would start alone, lifting up his whale-long tune
and at the right quaver, the rest set sail
after him, swaying, through eerie and lorn.
No unison of breaths-in gapped their sound.

In disdain of all theatrics, they raised
straight ahead, from plank rows, their beatless God-paean,
their giving like enduring. And in rise
and undulation, in Earth-conquest mourned
as loss, all tragedy, drowned, and that weird
music impelled them, singing, like solar wind.

                    Les Murray

DAT TRICKSTER SUN

. . . ee day he fills your window wi shaeps
o laands at you could mak your ain:
islands beyond islands, draemscapes
you could aa but map: a refrain o

licht troo a peen o gless; incongruities,
tizin places you'll nivver win tae.
You're stuck i da here an noo;
der oot o rekk, maist lik infinity.

. . . ee day he tirls a rainbow deep intil
anidder een. Cringed, dey rin wi you.
You could aa but lay a haand apo dem,
licht troo silence: a holy hubbelskyu,

da foo spectrum o taer-draps; a slow air
ta turn you inside oot, ta brak a haert.

Christine De Luca

dat: that; *ee(n)*: one; *shaeps*: shapes; *ain*: own; *aa*: all;
troo: through; *peen o gless*: windowpane; *tizin*:tempting;
win tae: reach; *der*: they are; *rekk*: reach; *tirls*: whirls, upturns;
intil: into; *anidder*: another; *cringed*: twinned, as on a conjoined
tether; *rin*: run; *aa but*: almost; *apo*: on; *hubbe/skyu*: uproar;
foo: full; *air*: melody; *brak*: break

GIGHA

That firewood pale with salt and burning green
Outfloats its men who waved with a sound of drowning
Their saltcut hands over mazes of this rough bay.

Quietly this morning beside the subsided herds
Of water I walk. The children wade the shallows.
The sun with long legs wades into the sea.

W.S. Graham

THE CALLANISH STONES

July. Summer on the island
muffles in scarves.
Merino-socked, Berghaus-booted,

swap cocoon of car
for hilly slither. Pilgrim-trail
with sodden strangers,

step in time to the cadence of rain.
White-trainered Americans patter: *there isn't a bus,*
Earl, I can't believe there isn't a bus.

Even taped seams leak. Cold as
Lewisian gneiss, circle
the circle of Neolithic ritual.

Reach out, for Callanish grants
what Stonehenge forbids:
it feels like wet stone.

On the downhill squelch,
the final syllable's a sneeze.
I buy a fridge magnet.

Nikki Robson

LIGHTHOUSES

Pladda: 3 white flashes per 30 secs; Lady Isle: 4 white flashes per 30
secs; Ailsa Craig: 1 white flash per 4 secs. *Northern Lighthouse Board.*

Tonight a milky misty sea
as if this soft grey day
is drained;
amber rose and gold funnelled
to blaze from lichen, seaweed, old rocks,
the moon still a wispy question
in a pale sky, back-lit by an unseen sun.
The sea has hidden its islands
Pladda, Lady Isle, Ailsa Craig,
Holy Isle, even Arran,
though its peaks are reprieved
Japanese-blue, sharpened brush strokes,
the only clue that darkness is falling;
and that from small clusters of rock
with the same certainty as sunrise,
light, white, always white will shine; sifting
safety from danger,
solitude from loneliness.

Sheila Templeton

A LANGUAGE OF NIGHT

The stone moon
is a night older than full
and the skies are occupied
with the transport of stars.
The wind drops to a breath
– a baby's breath;
the anchorage calms to a pond
– a summer pond;
the row-boats call across the bay
– the desolate oratory of oars.

It is worth being here for this alone.

In the slap of wavelets,
in the flap of sails,
and in the lilac stillness of harbour waters,
I heard Gaelic . . .

and the moon and the scars
and the waves and the sails
and the waters of this storied otherworld
whispered in that soft, sad sea-tongue
(and daughter, I gift you this mystery)

Leave your heart on this island forever,
waiting, waiting, waiting
– waiting for seals to show.

                                    John Rice

IV. LOVE AND LOSS

THE HOUSE BY THE SEA, ERISKAY

This is where the drowned climb to land.
For a single night when a boat goes down

soaked footprints line its cracked path
as inside they stand open mouthed at a fire,

drying out their lungs, that hang in their chests
like sacks of black wine. Some will have stripped

down to their washed skin, and wonder
whether they are now more moon than earth –

so pale. Some worry about the passage,
others still think about the deep. All share

a terrible thirst, wringing their hands
until the seawater floods across the floor.

Niall Campbell

A ST KILDA LAMENT

It was no crew of landsmen
Crossed the ferry on Wednesday;
'Tis tidings of disaster if you live not.

What has kept you so long from me?
Are the high sea and the sudden wind catching you,
So that you could not at once give her sail?

'Tis a profitless journey
That took the noble men way,
To take our one son from me, and from Donald.

My son and my three brothers are gone,
And the one son of my mother's sister,
And, sorest tale, that will come or has come, my husband.

What has set me to draw ashes
And to take a spell at digging
Is that the men are away with no word of their living.

I am left without fun or merriment
Sitting on the floor of the glen;
My eyes are wet, oft are tears on them.

Anon.

A WESTRAY PRAYER

i.m. Mike and Barbara Heasman

Let us now give thanks
for these salt-blown

wind-burned pastures
where outgrass and timothy
shrink from the harrow of the sea

where Scotland at long last
wearies of muttering its own name
where we may begin

to believe we have always known
what someone in his wisdom
must have meant

when he gave us everything
and told us nothing.

John Glenday

FINDING YOU IN RACKWICK

In Rackwick bay, stones are pink
with the effort of smoothing so much time
into perfectly flawed roundness.

They lie in a colony,
a petrified spawn of dinosaurs' eggs.
And from this distance the cliffs are tame,

postcard pretty. A fulmar
wheels from its nest,
tilts the world away from the sun.

A distant speck
jumps through the binoculars,
detaches from the steep and slatted rock,

becomes a little figure, running;
a tiny chaos making for an open shore.

Pamela Beasant

LOVE-MAKING IN ST KILDA

When a man makes love to a St Kildan woman,
her moans and sighs are like the cries of birds –
a cooing and screaming that seems scarcely human
but has been fashioned never to disturb
those who might mistake the sounds their passion makes
for flocks circling Village Bay at night.
Scanning skies for wings when morning breaks,
neighbours wake unaware that soaring flight
had taken place in Main Street's walls
as a man and woman coupled to break free
from an island's bonds and strictures, all
that conspired to tie them down. Gravity
was shed along with trousers, skirt and shawl
as they touched the heights the birds could reach
with their bodies' power and beauty, rise and fall,
arms charged to wings by the tumultuous air they breathed.

Donald S. Murray

THE TWELVE PIERS OF HAMNAVOE

Those huge apostle feet
Stand in the ebb.
        Twice daily
The god of whale and iceberg
Returns with gulls
To lay green blessings on them

Or spreads his wounds around
Threatening the nets

Or like an old blind ghost
Folds them in love and lost voices.

George Mackay Brown

LOST AT SEA

A herring-gull tears
on a roadside rabbit
at Lunabister.
Thin islands blow
like streamers off
the coast.
The custodian at Boddam
looks past me for
his view of voe
and surnames lost
at sea. Invisible
from here, in haar,
Garthsetters and Mansons,
Leasks and Mouats.
There used
to be Aikens at Ness,
Aikens at Ellister.
Once they were on Burra-Isle.

I'm reading graves at Papil.
Rub tough rain of lichen
off grey stone. 'William
Aiken who with crew
was drowned
March 12th 1866'.
I straighten up to find
the view his widow had:
the stones, the green,
the graves, the grazing

sheep. Invisible
from here, the sea
is sweeping up the voe
between the Burras.

Jean Atkin

THERE WILL BE NO END

There will be no end to the joy, my love.
We will stand together as the stars
sweep the Cuillen, rounding into morning
the bright new morning of the tender heart.
And where we sing, the song will be a fine one
and where we dance our steps will never fail
to tap the spring of life, of love and laughter
timeless as stars, the wheeling, circling stars
that dance and sing, and sing and dance again:
and there will be no end
to the joy.

Anne MacLeod

LOVE LIKE THIS

there's more than one way to love
and god knows the first time
she came and lay down beside me

we trembled so much the radiator
pipes rattled and we had to inch
the bed away from the wall

it was bliss it was all the deer
and vines and doves and honey
all the songs of solomon saying

come away with me my love and
so we went – day stripped
of decorum old celtic crosses

starting to sway as the calmac ferry
ploughed from fionnphort to iona
white scarves in its steely wake

                    Alyson Hallett

BROUGH OF BIRSAY, ORKNEY

I watch the waves break like contractions
against the narrow causeway that joins me

to your father. I count the seconds between
each swell, each desperate centimetre. Head down

shoulders twisted, he muscles through the gusts.
Relentless. I close my eyes, see him as I saw you.

I tell him *It's time.*
Come home. Come home. Come home.

Aoife Lyall

CLESTRAIN: ORKNEY

Boyhood home of John Rae, Arctic explorer

On a cloud-stacked spring afternoon
you can hear how even the mildest wind
buffets your voice into a mourn-
ful staccato, how words are thinned

down to their roots. Yet his voice
rasped through the elements, on the edge
of each curt order, a savage
delight in hardship. At the *noust* –

the cleft of rock where his sailboat
was once snug – I turn from the shore
and, cleaving to a dyke for shelter,
take the track to the sensibly squat

house of Clestrain. Here the wind's cut
and the stones tell only of absence,
broken by a last pigeon caught
fluttering out one more vacant lens.

There's a skeleton grandeur still –
the curled ironwork that lurches
from the staircase – a dainty school
indeed for the man who marched

till his moccasins were blood-shod;
who made soup from rotting fish-bones
and claimed you knew nothing of food
till you'd drained the last juices down

from a ptarmigan's toes. The thoughts
spool on, with a creak from a board,
a scuffed stone; a vision that rots
in the silence: the place can't hoard

the man. Out in the minch, a boy
hauls on a flapping sail, careless
of weather. Rain shushes like a sleigh;
flinty waves strain in their tresses.

But the boy looks past the cloth he holds
to the horizon's sudden silver:
beyond which lies death – or adventure –
and over which the stories roll.

Tom Pow

ISLAND WEDDING

It is an Islay evening and the winds
from the Atlantic have grown still
and the September sun is letting
go, reluctantly, its last clasp of the hills.

Beneath the slopes of divided fields,
the coupled dead lie hollowed in order
behind dry stoned walls, their long sleep
lulled by the black cattle's lowing.

A path leads through woods to the church,
where elm branches are shaken by the glistening
wings of rooks who call out and call
out to each other with deep voices,

crossing and re-crossing the flowered
gravel with their shadowed flight paths
like those intricate, unbroken
lines chiselled on Kildalton Cross.

Sunlight melts into the fires of sunset
and is reduced to ashes of dusk, then candles
flame from within, making stained figures on
glass dance their way into the darkness.

When the vows have been vowed and
the hymns have been sung and the toasts
all consumed, we make our way past Loch Indaal
on whose moon-enamelled surface, two mute

swans fold their separate wings
into a single, moving image of themselves
with Port Charlotte and Bruichladdich
reaching out glowing fingers to touch

Bowmore, where men stand still beneath lamps
at corners, haloed by light pools like Rembrandt's
nightwatchmen: we steal past them, gathering
as we go, ringed handfuls of low-slung stars.

James Knox Whittet

AN ISLAND DROWNING

You were the first death I ever shook hands with:
a practice death to toughen me up;
a shock, a punch in the gut,
and for months afterwards
I'd dream you'd arrive at school assemblies
to incredulous applause:
It's Fergus! He's survived! A miracle after all . . .
but we were both fifteen
and I hardly knew you at all.

That never stopped us French kissing though.
It was the mistletoe rule of the school Christmas dance;
strict and unbroken. You were shorter than me
and your lips were soft and full,
like segments of satsuma;
your freckles still visible in the disco lights.
Later, you told the other boys I bit you.
They sang the music from *Jaws*
when I walked the corridor.
I was strong enough to carry the infamy;
able to forgive you
your Dastardly and Muttley laugh.

On the homeward ferry we heard
your boat was missing; the sea slate calm,
a July sky slung low with aluminium rain clouds.
Did you have a lifejacket on?
I prayed for a tangerine dot
on an isolated rock,
the helicopter's rope drop.

We were back at school when your body washed up
on the beach where we swam the week before.
We said little but secretly wondered
what state you were in;

exhaled relief
that we were not the ones to find you.
There were whispers of fish scarring your skin,
kissing at your eyes
and your lips, soft and chilled.

Ciara MacLaverty

HEBRIDEAN FUNERAL

Black-clad they traik
ahint the semple pine kist
heids doon, een oan the grund
schauclin wi him tae the grave.

The watter skelps this dreich
shore and seamaws
greet fur mair, fur mair
abin the wave's rair.

Anither age caws them, bit
they haud oan tae custom
and cairry him tae the
heidland o his cauf kintra.

Nae greetin, nae wirds, stiff
moos howkit fae this dreichness
as they lower the kist
inch by inch intae the daurk.

The wind sears them
an they haund back the boady
tae its hame. The grund
pulls him intae her waim.

Ann MacKinnon

THE MOTHER TELLS HER DAUGHTER
OF A STORM

One night, when your Dad was out in the boat
in the worst gale I remember, I looked round
and there they were – all those fisherwomen
who'd waited for their men while the sea
spun up and slates crashed from the roofs.
The women sat, reasoning then pleading
with the sea to give the fathers back,
holding the babies up as human prayers.
The lighthouse women were there too,
wearing their white aprons, thinking if if if
and promising their hearts as solid faith
in exchange for the keepers – fourteen miles out,
tending the one light of the Torran rocks.
The women sat with me, as if they hadn't done
enough of this when they were alive
and I held you up to calm them, under the lamp.

Miriam Nash

V. CREATURES

HAULING-OUT

The ferry has brought me this far, slow,
rocking gently on its patches

of salt-rust, its bellyful of cars.
Cormorants are drying their wings

like dark angels resting from the hunt. Humpback
mountains dusted with snow

fall over themselves to fill the horizon,
or are caught, mirrored in the loch's dark shimmer.

Later, along the wet coast road,
I watch seals blubber onto boulders,

heavy bellyfuls of fish, and envy them their balance,
the way they rock gently on the point between two worlds.

Samuel Tongue

AILSA PAURIT/THE PUFFIN

The Ailsa Paurit gairds the Craig
in snaw-white downie tabart
a pirate coat upon his back
an cutlass in his scabbart.

Huffin an puffin amang the gress
it widdles then it scurries
wi colourt neb tae brod an jeb
the seamaw frae the burraes.

High on the sea-girt curlin stane
Wi cruin an gurly greetin
Feedin on the Tammie-yaw
Whan simmer tides are fleetin.

                    Hamish MacDonald

AT KILBRIDE

Sea-sculpted rocks on the beach
have the forms of languorous animals.

Bedded on white sand, three
cows with calves are chewing the cud.

Only the attendant starlings are busy
and a Ringed Plover, anxious on its rock.

But the tide is edging up the beach
gently tumbling its detritus:

pink fronds, intricate as frost,
scraps of carragheen and claret dulse.

And lifting wrack is offering secrets –
that retreat into lucid obscurity.

Out on the Sound the light is quietly
shattering on a resilient ripple.

The cows are shifting. They pause along
the road, tongues tearing at the verges.

Heads lift as you pass, eyes
fathomless, lost in their mystery of tides.

Henry Marsh

PERFECT

On the Western Seaboard of South Lewis

Los muertos abren los ojos a los que viven *

I found a pigeon's skull on the machair,
All the bones pure white and dry, and chalky,
But perfect,
Without a crack or a flaw anywhere.

At the back, rising out of the beak,
Were domes like bubbles of thin bone,
Almost transparent, where the brain had been,
That fixed the tilt of the wings.

Hugh MacDiarmid

* The dead open the eyes of the living

THE YOUNG MAN OF HOY SAID TO
HIS OLD MAN

Hey, Dad,

You'd get stacks of street cred
if you'd do as I say.

Façade retention is the latest thing.

You could become an eighty-feet-high
top-class restaurant.

Kit out your interior with
high rec steel, tubular chrome,
be an ultra-modern superstructure of
combined and compressed
melamine filaments of polyurethane PVC.
A towering lookout over the
North Sea, Pentland Firth and
from the top 16th floor, the
Irish Sea, maybe.

You could serve up a stushie
with your fresh organic sushi
local fish, sun-dried veg.

It would go down a storm up here,
with wind surfers.

How about a glass-topped dome looking out to the sky?

Birds, gannets, seals,
maybe a dolphin or two.
Imagine the sunsets, the Aurora Borealis,
light not fading all summer, the clear pure air.

Come on Old Man, why have you nothing to say?

Liz Niven

POSTCARD FROM AN ISLAND

the birds
at first they bothered me
so big
so strange
their cries.

just who
is that cuckoo
getting at all day?
the mechanical lark
on its yoyo string
the crossbow shadow of the hawk.

only took
two hooligan gulls
to chase that eagle round in circles
for half an hour before
they shot off yammering
to lord it at the tip.

big hoody
ugly bird
came down twice
sat square in the kitchen window
went caw caw
bashed his great horny beak twice hard
against the glass.

as if we were in an egg
big hoody was determined to smash
but seems there's no omen in it.

hoodycrow's only
a bird
who's looking for a mate
and fallen for his own reflection
you know how people get.

                    Liz Lochhead

THE GREAT SILKIE OF SULE SKERRY

An earthly nourrice sits and sings,
And aye she sings, 'Ba, lily wean!
Little ken I my bairn's father,
Far less the land that he staps in.'

Then ane arose at her bed-fit,
An' a grumly guest I'm sure was he:
'Here am I, thy bairn's father,
Although that I be not comèlie.

'I am a man, upo' the lan',
An' I am a silkie in the sea;
And when I'm far and far frae lan',
My dwelling is in Sule Skerrie.'

'It was na weel,' quo the maiden fair,
'It was na weel, indeed,' quo' she,
'That the Great Silkie of Sule Skerrie
Suld hae come and aught a bairn to me.'

Now he has ta'en a purse of goud,
And he has pat it upo' her knee,
Sayin', 'Gie to me my little young son,
An' tak thee up thy nourrice-fee.

'An' it sall pass on a simmer's day,
When the sin shines het on evera stane,
That I will tak my little young son,
An' teach him for to swim his lane.

'An' thu sall marry a proud gunner,
An' a proud gunner I'm sure he'll be,
An' the very first schot that ere he schoots,
He'll schoot baith my young son and me.'

And she has wed a gunner guid
A gey guid gunner it was he
And he went oot on a May morning
He shot the son and the grey silkie

'Alas, alas this woeful fate
This weary fate that's been laid on me'
She sobbed and sighed and bitter cried
Her tender hert did brak in three.'

                              Trad.

FROM ANOTHER ISLAND

They pulled him from the sea out at Mol Eighre
on a cauterised Sunday afternoon – the menfolk
in starch black, the women flattened hats,
on their way back from the English service.

The Balaich Aigh went in to their knees,
saltwater singeing their calves, and steered
his body gently to the shore, untangled
the hair-haul and with the tender horror of a parent

lifted him over the wrack to the stones.
He was naked but for the rough bounds
holding his hands behind him, moulding
his legs together into a tail at the ankle.

A linen sheet was found to spare their shame.
It was Iain Mhurchaidh that recognised him as
his own great-great-grand father
lost at sea over a century ago

Murchadh Beag Iain Sheonaidh Alec.
The brine had kept his skin, turned his innards to aspic
and by some god-awful miracle
returned him intact to the island.

It has not been talked on since.
Too vivid still his sea-swollen dick
and blue-tinged on the map of his back
the imprint *homines caudati hic.* (*)

Peter Mackay

.

(*) Here live men with tails. ('From the ever gullible Pliny to the openly
fictitious Marco Polo, travelers and writers claimed that tribes of humanity
bearing tails could still be found – in faraway locales, of course.' – Michael Sims.)

ARRAN

Arran of the many stags,
The sea strikes against her shoulder;
Isle in which companies are fed,
Ridges on which blue spears are reddened.

Skittish deer are on her peaks,
Mellow blaeberries on her heaths,
Cool water in her streams,
Mast upon her brown oaks.

Greyhounds are there and beagles,
Brambles and sloes of the dark blackthorn,
Her dwellings close against the woods,
Deer scattered about her oak-woods.

Gleaning of purple lichen on her rocks,
Flawless grass upon her slopes;
Over her fair shapely crags
Noise of dappled fawns a-skipping.

Smooth is her level land, fat are her swine,
Bright are her fields,
Her nuts on the boughs of her hazel-wood,
Long galleys sailing past her.

Delightful it is when the fair season comes,
Trout under the brinks of her rivers,
Seagulls answer each other round her white cliff;
Delightful at all times is Arran!

Anon.
*(Translated from Gaelic by
Kuno Meyer)*

THE MINISTER SEES THE MONSTER

It was a wet summer:
the village a damp fort surrounded
by field water. Four o'clock I was up –
the grey light punched and wrung –
like it had called me, like it needed to be seen.

I'm not a walker, but with stick and boots
and picked-thin overcoat I went.
Under the backfiring streetlights,
over the green with the dawn sky
turning like milk.

By the chapel the river was loud.
By the dyke the path was addled
with the glyphs of many hooves.
In the hedge birds quipped and flinched.
My boots turned black in the damp.

I cut round a ditch loosed
and pooled by rain.
On Cemetery Road
there's a gate I climbed,
slipping, giggling adrenaline.

Though it made no sound I turned there,
the old, hot wire of fear pulled taut,
and saw it through the blown thorns
for a moment. Long enough to know
that it was grey, and larger than a dog.

I inferred teeth. I cut home through the graves
for cover, wet white fog rising
round the houses like a useless keep.
I haven't told the village. I believe
whatever comes is what's deserved.

                        Claire Askew

THE MOON JELLYFISH

We find them melting
by the shoormal, like dropped

scoops of translucent ice-cream,
the same morning

of the old fisherman's funeral
at the chapel by our beach.

We'd seen the coffin going past
in a parade as slow as shadows

cast by summer clouds,
into the churchyard where

blind headstones watched us
playing daily with the waves.

The beach is filled with dead things.
Except the jellyfish.

We know they are immortal,
so when storms bring them

to the shore it is the saddest sight –
at least, that's what the fisherman

said. We want to save
the jellyfish. They ooze

between our fingers as we wade
out to the shallows, toss each

into the softly crooning waves.
Some have purple crescent moons

inside them; we think
they are the girls.

We do not know
the jellyfish are folklore,

a myth we're offering
the tide to be rejected:

for the dead will continue
being dead.

No; we know only the morning
deepening in the spaces

between pebbles, and the jellyfish
returning, dream-like, to shore.

Roseanne Watt

HONEYBEE, INNER HEBRIDES

We sail to the Garvellachs with an autumn wind
along the string of islands. Heading out over the waves,
a honeybee lands on the guardrail of the yacht.
Ginger-brown and banded, he is a lost forager

who travels with us, resting to regain strength.
Where the gap is navigable, we put in at a place
of sheltered creek and grassy hollow. A few steps
and we drink at the miraculous well of sweet water

dashed by salt spray. The beehive cells nearby
are circles of stone, overlapping slabs, a domed roof.
It takes a whole rocky island to make a single drop
of honey. How far to fly? A solitary bee arrives

who grips the hazel-rod rim of a coracle, till he flies
up and off rapidly, to find the golden honeycomb.

Valerie Gillies

THE BIRDS DREAM OF UIST

Oh the birds dream of Uist as they fly, as they fly
Uist of the singing lochs
Uist of the shorelines
The birds dream of Uist as they fly

It pulls them in the wind
It is the heart of the wind
It does not mind, does not mention
All the ground work, the vigilance
The pecking
It seals the lock in the air that
Keeps the flock exposed
Keeps it flying over shelter, further on
For the rest and the water at the end
Will be home

Head there
Finish there
Rest there
Nest there

Oh the birds dream of Uist as they fly, as they fly
Uist of the singing lochs
Uist of the shorelines
The birds dream of Uist as they fly.

Catherine Eunson

VI. FROM AFAR

PHOTOCALL: LERWICK, 1898

Elizabeth Scott, who starched these collars and smoothed
these heads of hair, sits at the heart of this photograph.
She faded out before the War that claimed three sons.

There is Mackie, who played Mikado on the Lerwick stage;
Donnie – his twin – who half a world away in Adelaide
felt his death twinges; Peter, pilot out of the port of Leith;

Annie, the lonely girl; Laurence, solicitor's clerk;
Will, whose will caused chaos, leaving goods to be shared
by his surviving brothers' sons,

                or his brothers' surviving sons.

Jim settled in Queensland. Frank was shelled on the Somme.
Bertie, sailing south with Anzacs, died of wounds at sea.
Tom was blown up in Jericho with Allenby's men.

Bob, shipmaster on the Tasman Sea, married Florrie
who could not stand Australian insects. They found
safe harbour in Vancouver.

Not in the group, Sam, still unborn
who would sell cars in New South Wales, marry twice,
and learn to fly at sixty (his last mistake)

and complete Captain John Scott's family.
Eleven sons and one daughter, pictured here,
still with their journeys to make.

                    Laurna Robertson

AN I MO CHRIDHE/IONA IS IN MY HEART

An I mo chridhe, I mo ghràidh
        An àite guth manaich bidh geum bà;
Ach mun tig an saoghal gu crich
        Bithidh I mar a bha.

                    ascribed to Saint Columba

In Iona of my heart, Iona of my love,
Instead of monks' voices shall be lowing of cattle,
But ere the world come to an end
Iona shall be as it was.

                Trad.

Isle of my heart, Isle that it loveth so,
Where chaunts the monk, only the kine shall low;
Yet before Heaven shall wax and Earth shall wane,
Iona, as she was, shall be again.

                        Trans Mosse Macdonald
                        (Iona, 1879)

LOOKING WEST

I dream we are two Viking jarls today,
with simple action plans and strategies –
along the lines of take life by the throat;
travelling in thrall into high places
spying out these wide Hesperides

from Skye's blue jagged Cuillin
to Jura's rounded paps, Kintyre
and even far-off Arran's hazy peaks
and all the lateral wonders
of a world adjacent and between
the blest islands of the west:
Iona, Colonsay, Coll
and Tiree, the Uists,
Barra, Mingulay,
stretching into the blue,
with Staffa, Ulva, Eorsa nearer to
our vantage point of Mull's Ben More.

This summit is among the high points
of two lives. Mind how you go,
you two. Evade descent.
Postpone the parting handclasp.
Consider another golden moment
and reflect. Beyond this pinnacle
a setting sun declines
into the anecdotage of Valhalla
and the sea. For every thing
that rises has to ebb.

                    Gordon Jarvie

from **THE SAGA OF MAGNUS BAREFOOT**

In Lewis Isle with fearful blaze
The house-destroying fire plays;
To hills and rocks the people fly
Fearing all shelter but the sky.

In Uist the king deep crimson made
the lightning of his glancing blade;
The peasant lost his land and life
Who dared to bide the Norseman's strife.

The hungry battle-birds were filled
In Skye with blood of foemen killed,
And wolves on Tiree's lonely shore
Dyed red their hoary jaws in gore.

The men of Mull were tired of flight;
The Scottish foemen would not fight
And many an island girl's wail
Was heard as through the Isles we sail.

On Sanda's plain our shields they spy:
From Islay smoke rose heaven-high,
Whirling up from the flashing blaze
The king's men o'er the island raise.

South of Kintyre the people fled
Scared by our swords in blood dyed red,
And our brave champion onward goes
To meet in Man the Norsemen's foes.

> Björn Cripplehand
> by way of Snorri Sturluson
> (trans. Samuel Laing)

A DREAM OF THE DALAI LAMA ON SKYE

A summer wind blows the horn of Glen Brittle.
It's a hard walk, Black Cuillin
to his left hand; asks
the midsummer moon
setting over Canna, *what metaphors
does the market whisper?
If the hills changed shape
                   who would tell me?*
She shines on ditches choked
with yellow iris: butter-lamps
in a temple corner; a snail-shell
in his moonlit palm:
the golden dimple of an icon's smile.
                   He smiles too, notes
the private union of burn and sea,
as one by one, laverocks rise,
irises open. When no one's watching,
he jumps lightly onto Soay
and airborne seeds
of saxifrage, settled
                   on the barren Cuillin
wake into countless tiny stars.

                              Kathleen Jamie

THE CAIRGEN WEANS

O dinna ban the cairgen weans,
But meet them wi' a smile,
They come to seek the healing breeze,
That blaws o'er Arran Isle,
O let the shielan shield fae harm,
The puir wee orphans bairn,
An' let them in that kindly care,
Thy homely virtues learn.

We brought the pale wee cairgen bairns.
The cotters care to seek
And noo they play among the Glens,
Wi' roses on their cheek,
They lo'e the isle that gave them health,
An' sair wid be their pain,
If noo ye shut the cotter's door,
Upon the cairgen wean.

You see yon sturdy ploughman che'il,
Yon bonny bloomin' lass,
He whistles o'er the furrow'd fiel',
She sings among the grass,
He brings nae curse upon the soil,
Her song a blessing earns,
An' yet they came into the isle,
Twa orphan cairgen bairns.

O mither come an' plead wi' me,
Against the edict stern,
That bids the cotter steek his door,
An' ban the orphan bairn,
An' let the cairgen rhymer's lay,
Plead not with thee in vain,
Still let thy shielan shield an' bless,
The cairgen orphan wean.

James Paul Crawford

HOMESPUN

I met a man in Harris tweed
As I went down the Strand;
l turned and followed like a dog,
That breath of hill and sea and bog
That clung about the crotal brown.
And suddenly, in London Town
I heard again the Gaelic speech,
The scrunch of keel on shingly beach;
The traffic's never-ending roar
Came plangent from a shining shore;
I saw the little lochs where lie
The lilies, white as ivory;
And tumbling down the rocky hills
Came scores of little foaming rills.
I saw the crofter bait his line,
The children herding yellow kine,
The barefoot woman with her creel,
The washing-pot, the spinning-wheel,
The mounds thrown up by patient toil
To coax the corn from barren soil.
With buoyant step I went along
Whistling a Hebridean song
That Ian Og of Taransay
Sang to me one enchanted day.
I was a man renewed indeed
Because I smelt that Harris tweed
As I went down the Strand.

Helen B. Cruickshank

VISA WEDDING #1

Listen, hit's simple:

> in Orkney I'm English;
> in England I'm Scottish;
> in Scotland, Orcadian –

this glib-gabbit, mony-littit tongue
snacks at identity as tho hit wis
a gollach piecie sappit wi
the sweet-n-soor o BELONG.

> Like aw they ither sangsters I

ballad the islans fae the ceety,
buzz the ceety fae the islans,
birn frantic throu hydrocarbons

fer transatlantic jouks whar hame
is happit in bacon, fried on grits,
tursit in that muckle myndin n ma'd-on
ancestry hit's at lang n lenth hausable.

> Hey, haud me close, America:

mak me yer kiltie mascot,
mak me yer islan exotic,
mak me yer immigrant boy,

mowten me wi soothren sun n muntain
fir-sap n ser me on ice-cream,
unnest me, unnest me, shaw me vistas,
spreid me skinkin ower strath n hill-run.

Leuk, I growed-up dancin

the Gay Gordons tae Blanket on the Grund,
Strippit the Willow tae On the Bayou,
shauchled n spittit ilka wird o Hit the Road

Jack n nivver cam back nae mair, gie me
laund lots o laund, tak me hame tae the place
I belong, send me aff feriver but
I ask ye please, no more nae mair no more.

VISA WEDDING #2

Listen, it's simple:

    in Orkney I'm English;
    in England I'm Scottish;
    in Scotland, Orcadian –

this slippery, many-coloured tongue
snaps at identity as though it were
an insect morsel lathered with
the sweet and sour of BELONG.

    Like all the other songsters I

ballad the isles from the city,
buzz the city from the isles,
burn frantic through hydrocarbons

for transatlantic escapes where home
is wrapped in bacon, fried on grits,
bundled in so much memory and made up
ancestry it's finally huggable.

    Hey, hold me close, America:

make me your kilted mascot,
make me your island exotic,
make me your immigrant son,

melt me in southern sun with mountain
pine sap and serve me on ice cream,
unnest me, unnest me, show me vistas,
spread me thin across plain and valley.

Look, I grew up dancing

the Gay Gordons to Blanket on the Ground,
Stripped the Willow to On the Bayou,
shuffled and spat every word of Hit the Road

Jack and never come back no more, give me
land lots of la nd, take me home
to the place I belong, send me off forever
but I ask you please, nae mair no more nae mair.

Harry Josephine Giles

LADY GRANGE ON ST KILDA

'They say I'm mad, but who would not be mad
on Hirta, when the winter raves along
the bay and howls through my stone hut, so strong
they thought I was and so I am, so bad
they thought I was and beat me black and blue
and banished me, my mouth of bloody teeth
and banished me to live and cry beneath
the shriek of sea-birds, and eight children too
we had, my lord, though I know what you are,
sleekit Jacobite, showed you up, you bitch,
and screamed outside your close at Niddry's Wynd,
until you set your men on me, and far
I went from every friend and solace, which
was cruel, out of mind, out of my mind.'

Edwin Morgan

THE ITALIAN CHAPEL, ORKNEY

Even the Romanesque façade –
Santa Croce in eight-foot driftwood –
can't quite prepare us for this shift
of light, from cold Orcadian
to golden Tuscan radiance.

Painted bricks in the Nissen's vault
lodge in the throat like grief, and fake
marble takes us in – as walls
are meant to – out of the cold. Northern
winters taught them perfect brushwork.

On islands bare of trees, their calendar's
scored-out days stretched, perhaps,
to a memory of cypresses.
A neutral ocean tossed up scraps
of wood and metal they could use.

At first they stretched barbed wire across
the sanctuary, where mother and child
wait as they've always done,
and the colour of Mary's dress
is the sea that lies between.

I want to think they painted grief
away for a space, laying such shadows
on plaster-board that all their patterns
sprang to life, ran free; each linked relief
reaching from Lamb Holm to Italy.

Anna Crowe

*The Italian Chapel was built from two Nissen huts by Italian PoWs
at Camp 60, Lamb Holm, Orkney, in 1942–1943, and decorated by
Domenico Chiochetti and others.*

ON ERISKAY

Eighty years ago a camera pans
slowly across a Hebridean bay
imprisoning the place in its dark lens;
saving the moment for another day
to wonder at. Steeped in opacity
somewhere behind the lens a watchful man
steadies the shot. He rescues what he can.

Out of the world comes rock; comes water, still
in its incessant movement. People come
a little later, breaking from the whole
on wings of thought. The burden of a name
follows soon after, and is not quite the same
the world over. Into the film a voice
comes now, our best redemption and our vice.

The commentary drifts through crotal, rope;
from wool to waulking songs while Eriskay,
uncomprehending in its hopeless sleep,
its sleepless hopefulness, says nothing. Grey
and lonely, it replies to these R.P.
pronouncements on itself with rustling grass,
sheep cries, white breakers crashing as they pass.

Only occasionally will a wave
of muted speech be audible beneath
the island's background sough. When from the grave
of withered mouths it falters into breath
for seconds at a time, I lay my wreath
of nearly understanding. *Càit an robh
mo ghaol?* They had no word for yes or no.

Bha i air Èirisgeigh – but let it go.

Stewart Sanderson

Càit an robh mo ghaol? – Where was my love?
Bha i air Èirisgeigh – She was on Eriskay

RECONSTRUCTED HEAD OF A YOUNG WOMAN

(Shetland Museum)

I press my brow to cold glass –
two women, head to head:
your face tilts like a ship's prow
challenging the wind,
morning sky over the North Sea
in your salt-washed cheeks
and eager, blue-green eyes.
Your hair falls like mine
from a centre parting, though holds
no trace of grey in its peat brown sweep.
Five thousand years between us, and yet
not a moment, it seems – recognition
like that spark you'd know how to strike
from stone. Thought tugs at your mouth's harbour,
a half-smile about to slip its mooring into laughter.

Your skull lies beside you, mute echo,
shell-white in spotlit stillness every curve
and crevice mapped by expert – minds:
your mask their exquisite calculation,
more real to me than any excavated bone.

Did you sleep, wake, love and weep
in the dark air of honeycomb chambers
built by shores I've only glimpsed
from plane and car my – stay too short
and anyway, my timing out of season?
I want to know you, unknown woman,
walk with you the cliffs at Silwick,

tread the paths of Scalloway, hear
your language beat the air again
with skua, scart and arctic tern,
learn your life, those days that stretched
behind your step, and (though you couldn't guess
their end would come too soon) gave you
such a fearless gaze of hope.

Gerda Stevenson

YELL SOUND

I always looked out at the world,
and wondered if the world looked back at me,
standing on the edge of something,
on my face – the wind from the cold sea.

Across the waters were mirrors to see
faces that looked like me,
people caught between two places,
people crossing over the seas.

And it seemed from my croft –
with the old stones and the sheep,
and the sound of the songs in my sleep –
that the music of folk somewhere meets

on the edge of the place we would be.
I've lived through some hard times.
My face is lined; my body so frail.
I used to think I might be able –

when the river ran to meet the sea,
when the sun and moon shared the sky –
to look out as far as the eye could see,
and raise a glass to the girl looking back at me.

                            Jackie Kay

MY SON'S PHOTOGRAPH OF
SHELLS AT KILDONAN

washed by the sea
into this abstract rickle
of blues and whites
    mussels cockles whelks scallops
    the odd orange pebble

what draws your eye
is the scrunch of sand
caught in the boat
    of a mussel

it reminds you of the grains –
    found long after the holidays
      gritting the pages of a book
      getting under your nails
        in a trouser pocket –

that remind you
    with that slight stound
    of the heart

that remind you

Hamish Whyte

BIOGRAPHICAL NOTES

JAMES AITCHISON was born in Stirlingshire and educated at Glasgow and Strathclyde Universities. He and his wife lived in Gloucestershire for several years, before returning to Stirlingshire. His critical studies include *The Golden Harvester: The Vision of Edwin Muir*. He has been a poetry critic at the *Scotsman* and the (Glasgow) *Herald*. He won the 1992 Canadian Writing Wilderness award for the long poem 'Canada', which appeared in *Brain Scans*. Collections since his new and selected volume *Foraging* include *The Gates of Light*, *Learning How to Sing* and *Edges*.

CLAIRE ASKEW grew up in the Borders and has, since 2004, lived in Edinburgh. She is the author of *The Mermaid and the Sailors*, *This Changes Things* and *How to burn a woman*. She has won the Virginia Warbey Prize and the International Salt Prize for Poetry; and was twice shortlisted for the Edwin Morgan Poetry Award. *This Changes Things* was shortlisted for the Saltire First Book award, the Seamus Heaney Centre Poetry Prize and the Michael Murphy Memorial Award. She was the 2017 Jessie Kesson Fellow and, from 2017 to 2019, writer in residence at the University of Edinburgh.

JEAN ATKIN was brought up in Cumbria, with Shetland ancestors. Her most recent poetry publications are *The Bicycles of Ice and Salt*, about two long and long-ago journeys by bicycle, *Fan-peckled* (Fair Acre Press), based on the lost words of Shropshire, and *How Time Is in Fields*. Her poetry has won competitions, been anthologised and commissioned and featured on BBC Radio 4. She has been Troubadour of the Hills for Ledbury Poetry Festival, and was BBC National Poetry Day Poet for Shropshire in 2019. She works as a poet in education and community.

MEG BATEMAN was born and grew up in Edinburgh, and studied Gaelic then took her doctorate in Classical Gaelic religious poetry at the University of Aberdeen. She taught there before moving to Skye, where she teaches at Sabhal Mòr Ostaig. Besides her own collections, the latest being *Aotromachd agus Dàin Eile/Lightness and other Poems* and *Soirbheas/Fair Wind* and *Transparencies*, her editor/translator output ranges from *Gàir nan Clàrsach/The Harp's Cry* and *Scottish Religious Poetry from the Sixth Century to the Present* to a poems and songs selection titled *Bàird Ghleann Dail/The Glendale Bards*.

PAMELA BEASANT, originally from Glasgow, has lived and worked for many years in Stromness. In 2007 she was appointed the first George Mackay Brown Writing Fellow, and from 2011 to 2017 directed the Orkney Writers' Course for the St Magnus Festival. Her stage plays have been performed throughout Orkney, and she has published numerous information books for children as well as poetry, the latter including *Running with a Snow Leopard*; a collaboration with photographer Iain Sarjeant titled *Orkney: A Celebration of Light and Landscape*; and *The Crow in the Rear-View Mirror*.

NORMAL BISSELL, formerly a principal teacher of history in Motherwell, lives on Luing. He was a founder member of the Scottish Centre for Geopoetics in Edinburgh. He is anthologised in *These Islands, We Sing* and elsewhere. His first volume, *Slate, Sea and Sky, A Journey from Glasgow to the Isle of Luing*, contains photographs by Oscar Marzaroli. Fruitful collaborations with musicians include performances at An Tobar on Mull and at the Moray Arts Centre. In 2011 he collaborated in poetry events with the Tabula Rasa Dance Company, archaeologists and artists at the Pier Arts Centre in Orkney.

GEORGE MACKAY BROWN (1921–1996) was born in Stromness. After his time at Newbattle Abbey College and the University of Edinburgh he seldom left Orkney, the source of his inspiration and setting for the bulk of his distinctive poetry and prose. He won the 1988 James Tait Black Memorial Prize and the 1994 Scottish Book of the Year award; and *Beside the Ocean of Time* was shortlisted for the Booker Prize. An autobiography *For the Islands I Sing* appeared in 1997. His poetry output is garnered in *Orkney Pictures and Poems, with Gunnie Moberg* (Colin Baxter) and *The Collected Poems* (John Murray).

ELIZABETH BURNS (1957–2015) spent much of her life in Scotland before moving to Lancaster, where she taught creative writing. Her first full-length collection, *Ophelia and Other Poems* was shortlisted for the Saltire First Book of the Year award. Subsequent books were *The Gift of Light, The Lantern Bearers, Held* and, posthumously, *Lightkeepers* (edited by Gerrie Fellows and Jane Routh). Her love of pottery led to collaborations with ceramicists; painters she wrote about included Gwen John, Winifred Nicholson and Anne Redpath.

GERRY CAMBRIDGE has published six collections of poetry since 1995, the most recent being *Notes for Lighting a Fire* (2012) and *The Light Acknowledgers & Other Poems* (2019), both HappenStance Press. A lifelong interest in natural history informs much of his writing. In the mid-1980s he was one of the youngest-ever freelancers for the mass-market magazine *Reader's Digest*, and he founded the transatlantic magazine *The Dark Horse*, still Scotland's foremost poetry journal, in Ayrshire in 1995. After many years spent elsewhere, he now lives again on the North Ayrshire coast.

AONGHAS PÀDRAIG CAIMBEUL/ANGUS PETER CAMPBELL was born and brought up in South Uist. As a teenager he moved with his family to the Isle of Seil, attending Oban High School where, his English teacher was Iain Crichton Smith. A double honours graduate in Politics and History from the University of Edinburgh, he has worked as a journalist, broadcaster, actor and writer. He was nominated for a Scottish Bafta Best Actor Award in 2007, his collection *Aibisidh* won the

Scottish Poetry Book of the Year award in 2011, and his novel *Memory and Straw* won the Saltire Society Scottish Fiction Book of the Year award in 2017.

NIALL CAMPBELL is from the Outer Hebrides. His first collection, *Moontide* (Bloodaxe), won the Edwin Morgan Poetry Award and was a Saltire First Book of the Year. It was also shortlisted for, respectively, the Aldeburgh and Forward awards for Best First Collection. His second book, *Noctuary*, was shortlisted for the Forward Prize for Best Collection. A selection from both was published in 2016 as *First Nights*, as part of the Princeton Series of Contemporary Poets. He is currently writing a libretto for an opera to be performed by the BBC Philharmonic Orchestra. He lives in Fife.

THOMAS A. CLARK was born in Greenock. Much of his poetry reflects walking in the lonely terrain of the Highlands and Islands. In 1973, with the artist Laurie Clark, he started Moschatel Press, at first for small publications by Ian Hamilton Finlay, Cid Corman and others. Since 1986 he and Laurie Clark have run Cairn Gallery, specialising in Land Art, Minimalism and a poetic Conceptualism. After many years in the Cotswolds, they moved, in 2002, to re-open the gallery in Pittenweem. He has works in permanent collections world-wide, and the Scottish Poetry Library has a collection of his Moschatel Press publications.

ANGELA CLELAND is a poet and novelist. Her poetry collections are *Waiting to Burn* (Templar Poetry, 2006), *And in Here the Menagerie* (Templar Poetry, 2007) and *Room of Thieves* (Salt, 2013). Her third full collection, *Real Cute Danger*, will be published by Broken Sleep Books at the end of 2022. Cleland also writes science fiction under the name Cleland Smith, and her debut novel *Sequela* was named in the Kirkus Review's Best Books of 2013. To support her writing habit, she hosts writing workshops and small group seminars, and provides one-to-ones and mentoring services to poets through the Poetry School.

PADDY COFFEY (1856–1937) was born in Co. Kerry and on coming to Glasgow worked as a stevedore. He wrote for the 'Gossip and Grumbles' column of the *Evening Times* for twenty years until his death. But although the acknowledged poet of the city's dockland, he claimed 'he was not a great success at the business'. His poem here is from *Pickings from the Poetical Works of Patrick Coffey, the Glasgow Harbour Bard* (John Menzies).

SAINT COLUMBA (521–597), or Colmcille, on being exiled from Donegal landed with twelve monks on Iona and founded the Abbey, the mother church of Celtic Christianity in Scotland. The translation by Mosse Macdonald was Newdigate Prize Poem, Oxford, 1879. The prophecy may be seen as fulfilled by the Abbey's restoration, primarily through the efforts of the ecumenical Iona Community founded in 1938 by the Rev. George MacLeod, later Lord MacLeod of Fuinary.

JAMES PAUL CRAWFORD wrote this poem in the visitors' book of Arran's Lagg Inn, in 1850, on behalf of the pauper or orphan children ('cairgen weans') banned by the 11th Duke of Hamilton from coming to live with local families. It has been seen as 'displaying the same humanitarianism as some of Robert Burns's works', and 'paralleling those present-day politicians who attempt to brighten the image of our cities by forbidding 'mendicants' from begging in the streets'.

BJÖRN CRIPPLEHAND ('Knitted Nieve' or 'Clench-Hand') was an eleventh-century skald and court-poet to Magnus Olafsson, commonly known as Magnus Barefoot, King of Norway from 1093 till his death in 1103. His accounts of Magnus's conquest of Orkney and the Hebrides in 1098 were incorporated in *Heimskringla: Sagas of the Norse Kings* by Snorri Sturluson, historian, poet and politician, born in Iceland in 1179 and murdered by a political enemy in 1241. Travel writer/translator Samuel Laing (1780–1868) was from Papdale in Orkney.

ANNA CROWE is a co-founder of StAnza, Scotland's Poetry Festival. Her translations of the late Catalan poet, Joan Margarit, brought a Society of Authors Travelling Scholarship. His two final collections were published as *Wild Creature* (Bloodaxe, 2021). Her poetry has been translated and anthologised, received three PBS Choices/Recommendations, and is recorded for the Poetry Archive. *Figure in a Landscape*, in memory of her sister, won the Callum MacDonald Award. Her latest collection is *Not on the Side of the Gods* (Arc, 2019). Born in Plymouth, she went to school in Marseille, and lives in St Andrews with her husband, Dr Julian Crowe.

HELEN B. CRUICKSHANK (1886–1975) was born in Angus and attended Montrose Academy. After a spell in London and involvement in politics and women's suffrage, she returned to Edinburgh. In 1927 she became Hon, Sec. of the newly founded Scottish Centre of the P.E.N. Club, and was supportive of the leading literary lights of the day. Her first book of poems, *Up the Noran Water*, came out in 1934. In 1971 the University of Edinburgh awarded her an honorary MA and in 1976 a group of friends unveiled a plaque on Dinnieduff, her house on Corstorphine Hill. The following year her *Octobiography* was published.

LYNN DAVIDSON calls New Zealand, Australia, and Scotland home. 'An Tigh Seinnse' is part of the poem series 'Return to Islay' from *Islander*, her latest collection (Shearsman Books, Bristol, and Victoria University Press, Wellington, 2019). A member of the Edinburgh feminist poetry collective, she had a Hawthornden Fellowship in 2013 and a Bothy Project Residency in 2016; she won the Poetry New Zealand Poetry Award, 2020 and was the 2021 Creative New Zealand Randell Cottage writer in residence. Her essays have appeared in the *Poetry Review*, London, *Cordite and Text*, Melbourne, and *Sport and Verb*, Wellington.

CHRISTINE DE LUCA writes in English and Shetlandic, her mother tongue. She has had seven poetry collections published, most recently *Veeve*, and five bilingual volumes (in French, Italian, Icelandic, Norwegian and

English). She was Edinburgh's Makar for 2014–2017. She has collaborated with musicians and artists from Shetland and beyond: in *Another Time, Another Place* she responded to the work of artist Victoria Crowe. She has written and translated stories for children and recently completed a second novel. She is a member of Edinburgh's Shore Poets and of Hansel Cooperative Press, a small publisher based in Orkney and Shetland.

CATHERINE EUNSON, originally from Orkney, has lived in Huntly, Stirling, Edinburgh, Devon, London, Glasgow and Benbecula. Her children went to school in Benbecula, and the family all lived there for twenty years until 2016. She worked first as a music therapist and then in arts and education with various community groups and as an event promoter. She wrote, played and recorded music for Pauline Prior-Pitt's *North Uist Sea Poems* and will send you a CD for the price of the postage if you would like to hear it. In 2020 she published a poetry pamphlet called *Mend*.

IAN HAMILTON FINLAY (1925–2006), poet, short-story writer, artist, sculptor, gardener, moralist and cultural vigilante was born in Nassau in the Bahamas and came to Scotland aged six. After years in Glasgow, London and Perthshire he spent the winter of 1955–1956 on Rousay, then a spell in Edinburgh, setting up the Wild Hawthorn Press and launching the periodical *Poor. Old. Tired. Horse.* In 1966 he relocated to Stoneypath, Dunsyre, transforming it into Little Sparta, its classical temples, ponds and sculptures internationally renowned. His poetry ranges from *Glasgow Beasts, An a Burd haw, an Inseks, an, aw, a Fush* to *The Dancers Inherit the Party*. In 2002, he received a CBE.

ALISON FLETT was born in Edinburgh and for a number of years lived in Orkney. She was shortlisted for the 2005 Saltire First Book of the Year award, had poetry and short stories published, and performed her work on television and radio. Since moving to Adelaide in 2010 her poetry has appeared in a wide range of magazines and anthologies. She was awarded a grant to explore the nature of home and belonging. She is the poetry editor of *Transnational Literature*. Previous publications include *Restricted Vocabulary, Writing Like a Bastard* and *Whit Lassyz Ur Inty*.

MAGI GIBSON'S six poetry collections include *Wild Women of a Certain Age*, re-released in a twenty-first anniversary edition in 2021, and *I Like Your Hat* (2020), both from Luath Press. She has held three Scottish Arts Council Creative Writing Fellowships and one Royal Literary Fund Fellowship. She has been writer in residence in the Gallery of Modern Art in Glasgow, and reader in residence at Glasgow Women's Library. She is published widely in journals and anthologies, including *Modern Scottish Women Poets* (Canongate) and *The Edinburgh Book of Twentieth Century Scottish Poetry* (EUP).

HARRY JOSEPHINE GILES, a writer/performer from Orkney, lives in Leith. Their verse novel *Deep Wheel Orcadia* was a Poetry Book Society Winter Selection. *The Games* and *Tonguit* were between them shortlisted for the Forward Prize for Best First Collection, the Saltire Prize and the Edwin Morgan Poetry Award. They have a PhD in Creative Writing from the University of Stirling. Their show *Drone* debuted in the Made in Scotland Showcase at the 2019 Edinburgh Fringe and toured internationally, and their performance *What We Owe* was picked by the *Guardian*'s best-of-the-Fringe 2013 roundup, in the 'But Is It Art?' category.

VALERIE GILLIES is a poet whose books include *Each Bright Eye, Bed of Stone, The Ringing Rock, The Chanter's Tune, The Lightning Tree, The Spring Teller* and *The Cream of the Well: New and Selected Poems*. A former Edinburgh Makar, Royal Literary Fellow and an Associate of Harvard University, Valerie co-facilitates the creative writing workshops at Maggie's Centre, Edinburgh, and is a trainer with Lapidus Scotland. With the Orkney photographer Rebecca Marr, Valerie has produced *When the Grass Dances*, a collaboration on the theme of Scotland's wild grasses.

JOHN GLENDAY'S first collection *The Apple Ghost* (1989) won an SAC Book Award while both *Undark* and *Grain* were PBS Recommendations. *Grain* was also shortlisted for the Griffin International Poetry Prize and the Ted Hughes Award. His fourth collection, *The Golden Mean*, was shortlisted for the Saltire Scottish Poetry Book of the Year and won the 2015 Roehampton Poetry Prize. His most recent publications are *mira*, an artbook in collaboration with Maria Isakova Bennett; *Selected Poems* (Picador, 2020) and *The Firth* (Mariscat Press, 2020), celebrating the Firth of Tay. He lives in Carnoustie.

W.S. GRAHAM (1918–1986) was born in Greenock. In 1938, having served his time as an engineer, he spent a year at Newbattle Abbey. The recipient of an Atlantic Award in 1947, on moving to Cornwall he became during the fifties and sixties a key member of the St Ives artistic scene. His early work evokes Clydeside and the west of Scotland, while in *The Nightfishing* (1955) the sea and fishing are symbolic of the creative process. *Malcolm Mooney's Land* (1970) and *Implements in their Places* (1977) convey a human warmth, while reiterating the dilemma of communication. His *Collected Poems* appeared in 1979, and *The Nightfisherman, Selected Letters* in 1999.

YVONNE GRAY is a writer and musician who lives in Orkney. Her work has appeared in magazines and anthologies in Scotland, Slovakia, Australia and the US as well as in *Swappan the Mallimacks*, *In the Hanging Valley*, *The Hours* and *Reflections* – a collaboration with artist John Cumming shortlisted for the Callum MacDonald Memorial Award in 2013. Recently she has co-written a libretto with playwright Rachel Lampert for an opera, *We Wear the Sea Like a Coat*, by composer Sally Lamb McCune, premiered by Opera Ithaca in 2022.

ANDREW GREIG has written over twenty books of poetry, non-fiction and novels. A full-time writer, married to novelist Lesley Glaister, he lives in Edinburgh and Orkney. 'Shelter' comes from *Found at Sea*, a book of narrative and reflective poems arising from a rowdy sail into Scapa Flow to overnight on the abandoned island of Cava. *The Arctic Whaler* is a small open boat, skippered by Mark Shiner, friend and luthier. Greig's latest collection, *Later That Day* (Polygon) features a number of Orkney poems. His *This Life, This Life, his New and Selected Poems*, is from Bloodaxe.

JEN HADFIELD'S awards include the T.S. Eliot Prize for her collection, *Nigh-No-Place* (Bloodaxe). *The Stone Age* (Picador), explores neurodiversity. Having written a libretto for an opera produced by Music Theatre Transparant, she is keen to explore contemporary folk lyric. She was the Charles Causley resident in Autumn 2018, is Creative Writing / Teaching Fellow at University of Glasgow and teaches students of all ages and levels of confidence through a number of creative organisations. She is working on a collection of essays about Shetland, where she lives and where she is building a house, very slowly.

ALYSON HALLETT'S latest pamphlet is *Covid/Corvid*, co-authored with Penelope Shuttle. Other books include *Tilted Ground, Six Days in Iceland, Stone Talks, Walking Stumbling Limping Falling, Suddenly Everything* and *The Stone Library*. She has written for BBC Radio 3 and 4 and for the past twenty years curated *The Migration Habits of Stones*, a project that looks at migration and how stones move around the world. With work sited in many different countries, she continues to collaborate with sculptors and scientists, dancers and visual artists. She was recently appointed to the EarthArt fellowship at Bristol University.

LYDIA HARRIS lives in the Orkney island of Westray. Her pamphlet *Glad Not to Be the Corpse* was published by Smiths Knoll (2012) and *A Small Space*, its subject a child bog burial, clothing from which is displayed in Tankerness House, won first prize in the Paper Swans 2019 competition. In 2017 she held a Scottish Book Trust New Writers' Award. She hosts the monthly meetings of the Westray Writers, and the Westray Poetry Library is shelved in her porch. Her poems have appeared widely in magazines; and her first full collection is due in 2022 from Pindrop.

DIANA HENDRY grew up by the sea on the Wirral peninsula. She has published six collections of poetry, the most recent being *The Watching Stair* (Worple Press, 2018). She has been writer in residence at Dumfries & Galloway Royal Infirmary; a Royal Literary Fund Fellow based at the University of Edinburgh; a co-editor of *New Writing Scotland* and a tutor on courses at Arvon and Moniack Mhor. She is the author of more than forty books for children – *Harvey Angell* won a Whitbread Award and her young adult novel, *The Seeing*, was shortlisted for a Costa Book Award. She lives in Edinburgh.

KATHLEEN JAMIE, poet and essayist, was born in 1962. Her work concerns nature, travel and culture. Her poetry collections to date include *The Tree House*, which won the Forward Prize, *The Overhaul*, which won the Costa Poetry Prize, and *The Bonniest Companie*, which was the 2015 Saltire Scottish Book of the Year. Her non-fiction includes the trilogy *Findings*, *Sightlines* and *Surfacing*, all regarded as important contributions to nature/environment writing. She is presently the National Poet for Scotland.

ROBERT ALAN JAMIESON was born in 1958 into the crofting community of Sandness in Shetland. Since graduating from the University of Edinburgh he has held the William Soutar Fellowship, co-edited the *Edinburgh Review* and tutored creative writing at the Universities of Glasgow, Strathclyde and Edinburgh. His works include three collections of poetry, *Shoormal*, *Nort Atlantic Drift* and *Plague Clothes*, and five novels, *Soor Hearts*, *Thin Wealth*, *A Day at the Office*, *Da Happie Laand* and *macCloud Falls*.

GORDON JARVIE was born in Edinburgh, grew up in Glasgow and Troon, studied in Dublin, Indiana and Sussex University. He is now resident in Craill, in the East Neuk of Fife. In between working as editor, publisher and author, he has bagged two rounds of Munroes. He has published many poetry collections, among them *A Man Passing Through: Memoir with Poems Selected and New*; as well as books on grammar, golf, mythology and children's titles for the National Museums of Scotland. He is fortunate to have grandchildren who love to read.

JACKIE KAY was born in Edinburgh. Among her poetry collections are *The Adoption Papers*, *Off Colour*, *Darling*, *Fiere* and *Bantam*; and for children *Red*, *Cherry Red* which won the CLPE Poetry Award. *Trumpet* won the Authors' Club First Novel Award and the *Guardian* Fiction Prize. Other works include *Wish I Was Here* and *Reality*, *Reality* (short stories), and *Red Dust Road*, a memoir about finding her Nigerian father. She is currently Professor of Creative Writing at Newcastle University and Chancellor of the University of Salford. From 2016 to 2021 she was National Poet for Scotland.

LIZ LOCHHEAD, born in Motherwell, studied at the Glasgow School of Art and was for several years an art teacher. Her poetry collections include *Memo for Spring*, *Dreaming Frankenstein and Collected Poems 1967–1984*, *The Colour of Black and White: Poems 1984–2003* and *A Choosing: Selected Poems*. Stage plays range from *Blood and Ice*, *Mary, Queen of Scots Got Her Head Chopped Off* and *Dracula* to a Scots version of Molière's *Tartuffe*. She succeeded Edwin Morgan as both Glasgow Makar (2005–2011) and National Poet for Scotland (2011–2016). In 2015 she received the Queen's Gold Medal for Poetry.

MARJORIE LOTFI'S poems have appeared in journals here and in the US, and in *Best Scottish Poems 2021*, and been heard on BBC Radio Scotland and Radio 4. *Refuge* contains poems about her childhood in revolutionary Iran. She has been Poet in Residence at Jupiter Artland, Spring Fling and the Wigtown Book Festival and was commissioned to write *Pilgrim*, a sequence about migration between Iran and the US, for the St Magnus Festival. She founded the Belonging Project, on the experiences of refugees across Scotland, and is a co-founder and director of the charity Open Book. She won a 2021 James Berry Poetry Prize.

AOIFE LYALL was born in Dublin and educated at Trinity College, Dublin, St John's, University of Cambridge, and the University of

Aberdeen. Shortlisted for the 2021 Scottish National Book of the Year Awards, her debut collection *Mother, Nature* (Bloodaxe) explores the tender and tragic experiences of pregnancy and early motherhood. A guest curator for the Scottish Poetry Library and a guest editor for *The Butcher's Dog*, she is writing her second collection with support from the National Lottery through Creative Scotland. Lyall lives in the Scottish Highlands with her family.

NORMAN MACCAIG (1910–1996) was born in Edinburgh. He attended the Royal High School and studied Classics at the University of Edinburgh. *From Riding Lights* to *Voice Over* he published fourteen collections of poetry. After a career as a school teacher he taught creative writing at the University of Edinburgh, before being appointed a reader in poetry at the University of Stirling. He divided his life between Edinburgh and Assynt, the latter the location for much of his poetry. In 1985 he received the Queen's Gold Medal for Poetry. In 2005 Polygon issued *The Poems of Norman MacCaig*, with a CD of his selected readings.

HUGH MACDIARMID (C.M. Grieve) (1892–1978) was born in Langholm. After war service he settled in Montrose as a journalist, using his *Scottish Chapbook* (1922–1923) to promote the Scots language. A hand-to-mouth Shetland period is reflected in *Stony Limits*. Seen as Scotland's most influential and controversial writer of the twentieth century, he urged the regeneration of all aspects of Scottish literature and culture. His *Collected Poems* and voluminous prose constitute a formidable opus; while *A Drunk Man Looks at The Thistle* (1926), with its synthesis of braid or Lowland Scots and other sources, is generally cited as the masterwork of modern Scottish poetry.

HAMISH MACDONALD'S poetry has been published in various anthologies and publications. He is author of the novel *The Gravy Star* and has written several plays which have toured throughout Scotland. He was the first Scots Scriever at the National Library of Scotland from 2015–

2017, and his latest poetry collection *Wilson's Ornithology & Burds in Scots* (Scotland Street Press, 2020) features new poems in Scots set alongside the ornithological illustrations of pioneering Scottish naturalist Alexander Wilson (1766–1813).

SOMHAIRLE MACGILL-EAIN/SORLEY MACLEAN (1911–1996), regarded as bestriding modern Gaelic literature, was born on the island of Raasay. He was schooled on Skye and studied English at the University of Edinburgh. His career as a school-master, and latterly rector of Plockton High School, was interrupted by serving with the Signals Corps in North Africa during the Second World War; and he was wounded at El Alamein. His first book, *Dàin do Eimhir agus Dàin Eile*, was published by William MacLellan in 1943; and a collected edition by Carcanet/Birlinn in 2017. In 1990 he received the Queen's Gold Medal for Poetry.

PETER MACKAY/PÀDRAIG MACAOIDH is a poet, lecturer and broadcaster. He has two collections of poems, *Nàdur De (Some Kind Of*, 2020) and *Gu Leòr (Galore*, 2015), both published by Acair, and a pamphlet, *From Another Island*, with Clutag Press (2010). He writes in Gàidhlig and English, and his work has been translated into Czech, French, German, Irish, Occitan, Macedonian and Slovakian. Academic output includes *This Strange Loneliness: Heaney's Wordsworth* (2021) and *Sorley MacLean* (2011); he is a Senior Lecturer in Literature at the University of St Andrews, and has been an AHRC/Radio 3 New Generation Thinker.

GARRY MACKENZIE is a poet and non-fiction writer based in Fife. His poetry has been published in journals and anthologies including *Antlers of Water*, *Dark Mountain* and *The Clearing*. A recipient of a Scottish Book Trust New Writers' Award, he has won both the Robert McLellan Poetry Competition and the Wigtown Poetry Competition. His non-fiction book *Scotland: A Literary Guide for Travellers* is published by I.B. Tauris/Bloomsbury, and his book-length poem *Ben Dorain: a conversation with a mountain* is published by the Irish Pages Press.

ANN MACKINNON writes poetry in both Scots and English. In 2014 a New Scottish Writers' Award for writing in Scots enabled her to complete a pamphlet, *Nae Flooers* (Tapsalteerie), shortlisted for the Callum MacDonald Prize. She has four other pamphlets and has been published in the *Herald*, the *Scotsman*, *Northwords Now*, *Chapman* and *Lallans* as well as in various anthologies such the *FWS*, *Federation of Writers, Scotland*, *The SWC, Scottish Writers' Centre* and *New Writing Scotland*. In 2017 she was a runner up and, in 2019 joint winner in the McCash poetry competition.

CIARA MACLAVERTY was born in Belfast, grew up on Islay and lives in Glasgow. She has published short stories and two pamphlets of poetry: *Seats for Landing* and *Past Love in the Museum of Transport*. In 2006 'Peeled' was selected by Janice Galloway as one of the Best Scottish Poems of the year. A New Writer's Award from the Scottish Book Trust followed in 2017. Her commissions include poetry for Scottish Opera and the Edinburgh Book Festival. She has been blogging for twenty years and is currently working on a memoir.

ANNE MACLEOD lives on the Black Isle. A retired dermatologist, she travelled to Skye, Lewis, Shetland and Orkney for clinics, and this island experience greatly enriched her working life, as did her active engagement in Medical Humanities. She contributed to Routledge's much praised *Medical Humanities Companion* series. She has published two poetry collections: *Standing by Thistles* (Scottish Cultural Press), shortlisted for a Saltire First Book award, and *Just the Caravaggio* (Poetry Salzburg). Her novel *The Dark Ship* was nominated for Saltire and Impac awards.

RUARAIDH MACTHÒMAIS/DERICK THOMSON (1921–2012) was born in Stornoway and grew up in Lewis. After graduating from the University of Aberdeen and serving with the RAF, he studied at Cambridge and Bangor before becoming assistant of Celtic at the University of Edinburgh in 1948, then in 1963 Professor of Celtic at the University of Glasgow. As publisher and editor, through Gairm Publications and as first

Chair of the Gaelic Books Council, he shaped Gaelic publishing in the latter half of the twentieth century. Among his awards were the Ossian Prize (1974), the Oliver Brown Award (1984), the Derek Allen Prize (2000) and an honorary degree from the University of Glasgow (2007).

HENRY MARSH was born in Broughty Ferry and now lives in Midlothian. He began writing on the death of a friend, a Gaelic Bard, Donald MacDonald of South Lochboisdale. His first collection of poems was *A First Sighting* (2005). Nine others have followed, latterly *The Bedrock: Poems on Themes from the Great Tapestry of Scotland*, *Under Winter Skies: The Last Journey of the Great Marquis*, (Montrose) and *From the Lonely Shore*. He has read at the Edinburgh International Book Festival, at StAnza, and at Taigh Chearsabhagh, the Arts Centre in North Uist. He taught English and a bit of Philosophy at the Edinburgh Academy for over thirty years.

EDWIN MORGAN (1920–2010) was born in Glasgow, where he lived for most of his life, though his outlook was always international. Endlessly curious and inventive, he translated from a multitude of languages and wrote in a multitude of voices and forms – poems, plays, libretti, essays, reviews and much more. He retired from the English Department of the University of Glasgow in 1980. He was appointed Glasgow's Poet Laureate in 1999 and Scots Makar in 2004. Key collections are *The Second Life* (1968) and *Sonnets from Scotland* (1984). His *Centenary Selected Poems* was published in 2020 by Carcanet Press. His legacy is continued by the Edwin Morgan Trust.

DONALD S. MURRAY is a Gaelic-speaking poet, author, non-fiction writer and occasional dramatist raised in Ness, Lewis who now lives in Shetland. His first novel, *As the Women Lay Dreaming* about the Iolaire disaster of 1 January 1919 won the Paul Torday Memorial Prize for 2020. His latest works are the novel *In a Veil of Mist* and *For The Safety of All: Story of Scotland's Lighthouses*. Among his poetry titles are *Small Expectations* (Two Ravens Press, 2010), *Weaving Songs* (Acair, 2011) and the illustrated collection *The Guga Stone: Lies, Legends and Lunacies of St Kilda* (Luath Press, 2013).

LES MURRAY (1938–2019), regarded as the leading Australian poet of his generation, grew up in poverty on his grandparents' farm in Bunyah, NSW, a district he later moved back to with his own family. His many collections range from *The Ilex Tree* and *Dog Fox Field* (1990), both winners of the Grace Levin Prize for poetry and *Subhuman Redneck Poems* (1996), winner of the T.S. Eliot Prize for poetry, to the *Collected Poems* of 2018. He also wrote *Killing the Black Dog: A Memoir of Depression* (2011). He received the Australian Literature Society's Gold Medal and the Queen's Gold Medal for Poetry.

MIRIAM NASH was born in Inverness and spent her early years on the Isle of Erraid, off the coast of Mull. She was the first writer in residence at Greenway, Agatha Christie's summer home. Her debut poetry collection, *All the Prayers in the House* (Bloodaxe) won a Somerset Maugham Award and was runner up for the Edwin Morgan Award. Her recent pamphlet, *The Nine Mothers of Heimdallr* (Hercules Editions), re-tells the Norse creation myth with textile images by her own mother, Christina Edlund-Plater. She currently lives in northern Italy, where she works as a school librarian.

LIZ NIVEN'S poetry collections include *Stravaigin*, *Burning Whins* and *The Shard Box* (Luath Press, Edinburgh). Public art collaborations include text in stone and wood. The author of *Scots Dossier for European Bureau of Minority Languages*, she has edited a wide range of publications including *New Writing Scotland* (ASLS) and various education resources for poetry and the Scots language. Awards include McCash poetry prize, Saltire/TES. She is an Honorary Fellow of the Association for Scottish Literature and convener of Scottish PEN's Writers-in-exile committee.

TOM POW'S *Dear Alice, Narratives of Madness* won the Scottish Mortgage Investment Trust Poetry Book of the Year in 2009, the same year *In The Becoming – New and Selected Poems* was published. *In Another World: Among Europe's Dying Villages* was published in 2012. He edited *Barefoot: The Collected Poems of Alastair Reid* for Galileo Publishing (2018), which published his latest collection, *Naranjas* (2021). He has held several residences and his work has been recorded for the Poetry Archive. In 2019, he was Creative Director of A Year of Conversation. He is a lover of islands.

ALISON PRINCE (1931–2019) was born in Beckenham and educated at Goldsmiths, University of London and the Slade School of Fine Art. Among awards for her novels for young people was the *Guardian* Children's Fiction Prize. As a TV scriptwriter she contributed to *Jackanory* and wrote the series *Trumpton*. In 2005 she was awarded an honorary DLitt. by the University of Leicester for services to children's literature. Works for adults include biographies of Kenneth Grahame and Hans Christian Andersen. As well as poetry collections *Having Been in the City* (1994) and *The Whifflet Train* (2003).

PAULINE PRIOR-PITT is a poet and performer who has been living on the island of North Uist for the last twenty-three years. She has published seven collections and four pamphlets, including *Be an Angel: Selected Poems 1987–2017*. *North Uist Sea Poems* won the Callum MacDonald Award. Her poems about women, alternately funny and poignant, reflect their preoccupations and the juggling lives they lead. Her island poems, deeply rooted in the life of the Hebrides, take you to the sea and the shores close to her home. She regularly performs at poetry readings and festivals in Scotland and England.

JOHN PURSER is well-known as a composer, writer, lecturer and musicologist. He has published five collections of poetry, including most recently *There Is No Night* and *This Much Endures*, and his poems have appeared widely in magazines and anthologies. His radio play *Carver*, about Scotland's greatest composer, won a Giles Cooper Award, and his ground-breaking book *Scotland's Music* won the McVitie Scottish Writer of the Year Award. Purser is a researcher at Sabhal Mòr Ostaig, the Gaelic College on the Island of Skye, where he lives and crofts with his American wife, Barbara.

ALASTAIR REID (1926–2014), born in Whithorn, in Galloway, was one of the most international figures in post-war Scottish literature. A long-term staff writer for the *New Yorker,* he was an essayist, and translator of Latin American writers including Neruda and Borges. In the 1950's he worked with Robert Graves, in Minorca. He produced over forty books of poetry, prose, children's books and travel writings, including *Outside In* (selected prose) and *Inside Out* (selected poetry and translations), while *Barefoot: The Collected Poems* (Galileo) appeared posthumously.

ALAN RIACH, born in Airdrie, Lanarkshire, in 1957, is Professor of Scottish Literature at the University of Glasgow. He studied at Cambridge and Glasgow, and worked at the University of Waikato, New Zealand, returning to Scotland in 2001. His poetry includes: *Winter Book, Wild Blue: Selected Poems* and *Homecoming*; and criticism: *Hugh MacDiarmid's Epic Poetry* and *Representing Scotland*; and co-authored with Alexander Moffat: *Arts of Resistance: Poets, Portraits and Landscapes of Modern Scotland* and *Arts of Independence: The Cultural Argument and Why It Matters Most.*

JOHN RICE was born in Glasgow and grew up in Saltcoats. At eighteen he joined the British Army's Intelligence Corps and became an Arabic translator. After his army service he settled in Kent, as a literature officer for the Arts Council. He has published several collections of poetry for adults, among them *The Dream of Night Fishers: Scottish Islands in Poems and Photographs*, and edited the anthology *Scottish Poems* for Macmillan. His poetry collections for children, including *Zoomballoomballistic* and *Dreaming of Dinosaurs*, are widely used in schools.

LAURNA ROBERTSON'S poem identifies her grandfather, nine of his brothers, his sister and their parents, grouped for a formal studio portrait, in Lerwick in 1898. Donnie, who was at sea, is represented in a photo held by eight-year-old Tommy standing next to his mother's chair. The poem was published in *Praise Song*, (HappenStance, 2014), which is a memoir of growing up in Shetland, of the landscape and of her family. Other publications are *The Ranselman's Tale* (Shetland Publishing Company), *Milne Graden Poems* (Selkirk Lapwing Press) and *A Sampler* (HappenStance).

NIKKI ROBSON is from Northern Ireland and lives in Scotland. She holds an MLitt in Writing Practice and Study from the University of Dundee and her poems appear in journals and anthologies, both in print and online, including *Poetry Scotland*, *Acumen*, *Northwords Now*, *Under the Radar* and *The Lake*. She has previously been awarded first prize in the Elbow Room competition, been runner-up in Shooter Poetry Competition, and been highly commended at Wigtown and Carers UK.

DILYS ROSE lives in Edinburgh. She has published, most recently, *Unspeakable* (Freight, 2017), a fact-based historical novel, and a poetry pamphlet, *Stone the Crows* (Mariscat Press, 2020). *Sea Fret*, a collection of short stories, is forthcoming. For nearly twenty years she taught creative writing at the Universities of Glasgow, Strathclyde and Edinburgh and was a Royal Literary Fund Fellow at the University of Glasgow for three years. Since giving up teaching she has developed her visual art practice and during the pandemic produced a series of collages and ink drawings resulting in an online exhibition, *Waiting, Waiting*.

CHRYS SALT is a primarily a poet with roots deeply planted in the theatre. She has written four full poetry collections and five pamphlets, performed her work UK-wide, in the USA, Canada, France, Germany, Finland, India and Australia, and received many bursaries and awards. She visited Uist to research her collection *Grass*. In 2014 she received a Creative Scotland Bursary to finish *Dancing on a Rock* (Indigo Dreams Publishing) and another in 2016 to research her most recent collection about the Yukon Gold Rush. In 2014 she was awarded an MBE for Services to the Arts.

STEWART SANDERSON is a poet from Glasgow. Three times shortlisted for the Edwin Morgan Poetry Award (2014, 2016, 2020), he has also received an Eric Gregory Award (2015), as well as Robert Louis Stevenson (2016) and Jessie Kesson Fellowships (2019). Widely published in magazines and anthologies, he has performed internationally and participated in translation exchange projects with Friesland, North Africa and Russia. He is the author of two pamphlets – *Fios* (2015) and *An Offering* (2018). *The Sleep Road*, published by Tapsalteerie in 2021, is his first full-length collection.

IAIN CRICHTON SMITH (1928–1998) was born in Glasgow and grew up in Lewis. After studying at the University of Aberdeen, and two years of National Service, he taught in Clydebank and Oban, moving, after his marriage, to Taynuilt. Prolific in Gaelic and English, his output ranges remarkably from the elegance of his early poetry, and the Saltire Prize-winning *Collected Poems* of 1992, to a key translation of Sorley MacLean's *Dàin do Eimhir/Poems to Eimhir*; and from the poignancy of the first of his twelve novels, *Consider the Lilies*, to the zaniness of *Murdo: The Life and Works*. A revised and enlarged *New Collected Poems* came out from Carcanet Press in 2011.

KAREN SOLIE was born in Moose Jaw, Saskatchewan. Her four poetry collections include *Pigeon*, which won the Griffin Poetry Prize, the Pat Lowther Award, and the Trillium Award for Poetry, and *The Caiplie Caves*. She was the international writer in residence at the University of St Andrews in 2011. Her poems have been published in the US, the UK, Australia and Europe, and translated into French, German, Korean, Hebrew and Dutch. Her first UK collection was *Living Option: Selected Poems* (2013). She lives in Toronto.

IAN STEPHEN lives in Vatisker, Isle of Lewis. His first book of poetry was *Malin, Hebrides, Minches* (Dangaroo Press, 1983) and his most recent is *Maritime*, a selected volume on sea and coastal themes (Saraband, 2017). The British Council funded the translation into Czech by Bob Hysek of an earlier selected volume *Adrift* (Periplum, 2007). He continues to publish poetry in several countries. He is the author of a novel, *A Book of Death and Fish* (Saraband). *Waypoints* (Bloomsbury, 2017) was shortlisted for the Saltire Non-FictionBook of the Year.

KENNETH STEVEN is a full-time writer living on the Scottish west coast. He is first and foremost a poet: many of his collections have appeared in both Scotland and England, and in 2021 his volume of new and selected poems, *Iona*, was published by Paraclete Press in the US. Ten of his essays on Scottish islands were commissioned and produced by BBC Radio 3. His feature on St Kilda won a Sony Gold Medal some years back. He is also a novelist and children's author. He and his wife lead retreats on Iona each autumn.

GERDA STEVENSON, writer/actor/director/singer-songwriter, works in theatre, TV, radio, opera and film. Her plays include *Federer Versus Murray*, which toured to New York, and an opera libretto, *The Rime of the Ancient Mariner*, a contemporary retelling of Coleridge's poem. She received an MG ALBA Scots Singer of the Year nomination for her album of songs, *Night Touches Day*. Her poetry collections are *If This Were Real*, and *Quines: Poems in Tribute to Women of Scotland*, both also in Italian translation, *Inside & Out: The Art of Christian Small* and *Edinburgh*, with landscape photographer Allan Wright. She has also published a short story collection, *Letting Go*.

SHEILA TEMPLETON writes in Doric Scots and English. She has been Makar of the Federation of Writers (Scotland) and was nominated in 2020 for a Scots Writer of the Year Award. Her poetry has won top prizes, including the McCash Poetry Prize, the McLellan and Neil Gunn Poetry awards. She has recent work in *Owersettin* and *Drochaid*, collaborative publications by Tapsalteerie Press, and her own latest full collections are *Gaitherin* and *Clyack*, both Red Squirrel Press. *Norlan Lichts*, with two other north-east poets, is due in 2022.

SAMUEL TONGUE'S first collection of poems is *Sacrifice Zones* (Red Squirrel, 2020), and he has published two pamphlets: *Stitch* (Tapsalteerie, 2018) and *Hauling-Out* (Eyewear, 2016). A third, *The Nakedness of the Fathers*, was published by Broken Sleep in 2022. Poems have appeared in many places, including in *Banshee, Butcher's Dog, Magma, Finished Creatures*,

PBLJ, *Under the Radar* and elsewhere. His work has been translated into Latvian, Ukrainian, and Arabic. More details to be found at samueltongue.com.

ROSEANNE WATT is a writer, film-maker and musician from Shetland. Her dual-language debut collection, *Moder Dy*, was published by Polygon in 2019, after receiving the Edwin Morgan Poetry Award 2018. *Moder Dy* was subsequently named joint-winner of the Highland Book Prize 2019, and received both an Eric Gregory and Somerset Maugham Award in 2020. She has been editor of the online journal *The Island Review*. She also performs in the bands Lukkie Minnine and Wulver, where she plays fiddle, vocals and guitar.

JAMES KNOX WHITTET was born and grew up on Islay, his father being head gardener at Dunlossit Castle; and educated at Newbattle Abbey College and the University of Cambridge. He lives in Norfolk. Publications include *Seven Poems for Engraved Fishermen* and (as editor) *100 Island Poems of Great Britain* and *Ireland and Writers On Island*s. He won the George Crabbe Memorial Award on several occasions; and in 2009, the Neil Gunn Memorial Award for poetry. In 2012 he collaborated with an artist and photographer on an exhibition of sonnets, *Voices and Images of Islay*.

HAMISH WHYTE was born near Glasgow where he lived before moving to Edinburgh in 2004. *Paper Cut* (2020) is his fourth poetry collection with Shoestring Press. Among many anthologies he has edited are *The Scottish Cat*, *Mungo's Tongues* and *An Arran Anthology*, and he runs the award-winning Mariscat Press. He has been a librarian, indexer and crime fiction reviewer. For Edwin Morgan's centenary in 2020 he edited his *Centenary Selected Poems* (Carcanet) and published a memoir, *Morgan & Me* (HappenStance). He's a member of Edinburgh's Shore Poets and plays percussion and drums in a couple of bands.

The lines in praise of Arran are from *Agallamh na Senórach*, an anonymous thirteenth-century colloquy in Irish Gaelic. This translation is by Kuno Meyer (1858–1919), a Hamburg-born scholar regarded primarily as a lexicographer, who earned distinction in the field of Celtic philology and literature. As a teenager he spent two years in Edinburgh, learning English.

'A St. Kilda Lament', in which a woman mourns the loss of all the menfolk in her family in a tragedy at sea, was among the many lyrics drawing on the heritage of the people of the island collected by the folklorist Alexander Carmichael in 1865 from the St Kilda poet Euphemia MacCrimmon, eighty-four years old at the time, for the *Carmina Gadelica* for which Carmichael is principally remembered.

'The Great Silkie of Sule Skerry' was included by Captain F.W.L. Thomas, RN 'from the dictation of a venerable lady of Snarra Voe, Shetland', in *The Proceedings of The Society of Antiquaries of Scotland* I (1852), and later listed as 'Child ballad number 113'. Given renderings by folk-singers from Jean Redpath to Joan Baez, this tale of a doomed child has a heart-rending and haunting quality.

ACKNOWLEDGEMENTS

Thanks are due to the following authors, publishers and estates who have generously given permission to reproduce works:

James Aitchison, 'Islay Loch', from *Foraging: New and Selected Poems* (Worple Press, 2009), by permission of the author; Claire Askew, 'The Minister Sees the Monster', from *This Changes Things* (Bloodaxe, 2016), by permission of the publisher; Jean Atkin, 'Lost at Sea', from *Lost at Sea* (Roncadora Press, 2010), by permission of the author; Meg Bateman, 'Beinn Aslaig', from *Transparencies* (Polygon, 2013), by permission of the publisher; Pamela Beasant, 'Finding You in Rackwick', from *Running with a Snow Leopard* (Two Ravens Press, 2008), by permission of the author; Norman Bissell, 'Lone Seal Travelling South', from *Slate, Sea and Skye* (Luath Press, 2007), by permission of the author; George Mackay Brown, 'The Twelve Piers of Hamnavoe', from *The Collected Poems of George Mackay Brown* (John Murray, 2005), by permission of the publsher; Elizabeth Burns, 'At Barra Airport', from *The Gift of Light* (Diehard Poetry, 1999), by permission of the estate; Aonghas Pàdraig Caimbeul/Angus Peter Campbell, 'An T-Seann Chairt Againn/Our Old Cart', from *Aibisidh* (Polygon, 2013), by permission of the publisher; Gerry Cambridge, 'Shell Beach, Eigg', from *Notes for Lighting a Fire* (HappenStance, 2012), by permission of the author; Niall Campbell, 'The House by the Sea, Eriskay', from *Moontide* (Bloodaxe, 2014), by permission of the publisher; Thomas A. Clark, 'Creag Liath', from *The Path to the Sea* (Arc, 2005), by permission of the publisher; Angela Cleland, 'Blaeberries', from *Book of Thieves* (Salt, 2013), by permission of the author; Anna Crowe, 'The Italian Chapel, Orkney', from *Punk with Dulcimer* (Peterloo Poets, 2006), by permission of the author; Helen B. Cruickshank, 'Homespun', from *The Ponnage Pool* (Macdonald, 1968), by permission of Flora E.M. Hunter, the estate of Helen B. Cruikshank; Lynn Davidson, 'An Tigh Seinnse', from

Islander (Shearsman Books, 2019), by permission of the author; Christine De Luca, 'Dat Trickster Sun', from *Dat Trickster Sun* (Mariscat Press, 2014), by permission of the author; Catherine Eunson, 'The Birds Dream of Uist', from the StAnza poetry map, by permission of the author; Ian Hamilton Finlay, 'Fishing from the Back of Rousay', from *The Dancers Inherit the Party* (Polygon, 2004), by permission of the publisher; Alison Flett, 'Harbour', from *Whit Lassyz Ur Inty* (Thirsty Books, 2004), by permission of the publisher; Magi Gibson, 'Visiting Arran with My Mother', from *Washing Hugh MacDiarmid's Socks* (Luath Press, 2017), by permission of the author; Harry Josephine Giles, 'Visa Wedding #1 & #2', from *Visa Wedding* (Stewed Rhubarb, 2012), by permission of the author; Valerie Gillies, 'Honeybee, Inner Hebrides', from *The Spring Teller* (Luath Press, 2008), by permission of the author; John Glenday, 'A Westray Prayer', from *Grain* (Picador, 2009), by permission of the publisher; W.S. Graham, 'Gigha', from *Collected Poems 1942–1977* (Faber and Faber, 2005), by permission of Andy Ching, the estate of W.S. Graham; Yvonne Gray, 'Between the Terminals', from *In the Hanging Valley* (Two Ravens Press, 2008), by permission of the author; Andrew Greig, 'Shelter', from *Found at Sea* (Polygon, 2013), by permission of the publisher;' Jen Hadfield, 'Hydra', from *Byssus* (Picador, 2014), by permission of the publisher; Alyson Hallett, 'Love Like This', from *Toots* (Mariscat Press, 2017), by permission of the author; Lydia Harris, 'Scored with a Moon', from *The Island Review*, by permission of the author; Diana Hendry, 'Without Trees on Shetland', from *Borderers* (Peterloo Poets, 2001), by permission of the author; Kathleen Jamie, 'A Dream of the Dalai Lama on Skye', from *Mr and Mrs Scotland Are Dead: Poems 1980–1994* (Bloodaxe, 2012), by permission of the publisher; Robert Alan Jamieson, 'Frisk Waatir Troot', from *Nort Atlantik Drift* (Luath Press, 2007), by permission of the author; Gordon Jarvie, 'Looking West', from *A Man Passing Through: Memoir with Poems Selected and New* (Greenwich Exchange, 2016), by permission of the author; Jackie Kay, 'Yell Sound', from *Darling: New & Selected Poems* (Bloodaxe Books, 2008), by permission of the publisher; Liz Lochhead, 'Postcard from an Island', from *Dreaming Frankenstein & Collected Poems* (Polygon, 1984), by permission of the publisher; Marjorie Lotfi, 'Sunday on the Luing Sound', from *House of Three*

Vol I (Hybrid Press, 2016), by permission of the author; Aiofe Lyall, 'Brough of Birsay, Orkney', from *Mother Nature* (Bloodaxe, 2021), by permission of the publisher; Norman MacCaig, 'Wreck', from *The Poems of Norman MacCaig* (Polygon, 2005), by permission of the publisher; Hugh MacDiarmid, 'Perfect', from *Collected Poems of Hugh MacDiarmid* (Carcanet, 2017), by permission of the publisher; Hamish MacDonald, 'Ailsa Paurit/The Puffin', from *Wilson's Ornithology & Burds in Scots* (Scotland Street Press, 2020), by permission of the author; Peter Mackay, 'From Another Island', from *Gu Lòr/ Galore*, by permission of the author; Garry MacKenzie, 'Lewisian Nights', from *Scottish Book Trust New Writing 2009* (Scottish Book Trust, 2009), by permission of the author; Ann MacKinnon, 'Hebridean Funeral', from *Scottish Book Trust New Writing 2015* (Scottish Book Trust, 2015), by permission of the author; Ciara MacLaverty, 'Island Drowning', from *Seats for Landing* (Dreadful Night Press, 2005), by permission of the author; Somhairle MacGill-Eain/Sorley MacLean, 'Am Bàta Dubh/The Black Boat', from *White Leaping Flame: Collected Poems* (Polygon/Carcanet, 2011), by permission of the publishers; Anne MacLeod, 'There will be no end', from *Standing by Thistles* (Scottish Cultural Press, 1997), by permission of the author; Henry Marsh, 'At Kilbride', from *A Turbulent Wake* (Maclean Dubois, 2007), by permission of the author; Edwin Morgan, 'Lady Grange on St Kilda', from *Collected Poems* (Carcanet, 1990), by permission of the publisher; Donald S. Murray, 'Love-making in St Kilda', from *The Guga Stone: Lies, Legends and Lunacies from St Kilda* (Luath Press, 2013), by permission of the author; Les Murray, 'The Gaelic Long Tunes', from *New Collected Poems* (Carcanet, 2002), by permission of the publisher; Miriam Nash, 'The Mother Tells Her Daughter of a Storm', from *All the Prayers in the House* (Bloodaxe, 2017), by permission of the publisher; Liz Niven, 'The Young Man of Hoy Said to His Old Man', from *Burning Whins* (Luath Press, 2004), by permission of the author; Tom Pow, 'Clestrain, Orkney', from *In the Becoming, New & Selected Poems* (Polygon, 2009), by permission of the publisher; Alison Prince, 'Early Bus', from *Waking at Five Happens Again* (HappenStance, 2016), by permission of the estate; Pauline Prior-Pitt, 'Arrival of the Ferry at Lochmaddy', from *Be an Angel* (Spike Press, 2017), by permission of the author; John Purser,

'November from the Clach Rathad', from *There Is No Night: New and Selected Poems* (Kennedy and Boyd, 2014), by permission of the author; Alastair Reid, 'Isle of Arran', from *Inside Out* (Polygon, 2008), by permission of the Colchie Agency, the estate of Alistair Reid; Alan Riach, 'Vanishing Point', from *Homecoming* (Luath Press, 2009), by permission of the author; John Rice, 'A Language of Night', from *The Dream of Night Fishers* (Scottish Cultural Press, 1998), by permission of the author; Laurna Robertson, 'Photocall: Lerwick 1898', from *Praise Song* (HappenStance, 2014), by permission of the author; Nikki Robson, 'The Callanish Stones', from *Scotia Extremis* (Luath Press, 2019), by permission of the author; Dilys Rose, 'Eating Orkney', from *Lure* (Chapman, 2003), by permission of the author; Chrys Salt, 'The War', from *Grass* (Indigo Dreams Publishing, 2012), by permission of the author; Stewart Sanderson, 'On Eriskay', from *Fios* (Tapsalteerie, 2015), by permission of the author; Iain Crichton Smith, 'By Ferry to the Island', from *New Collected Poems* (Carcanet, 1992), by permission of the publisher; Karen Solie, '56.1833° N, 2.5667° W', from *The Caiplie Caves* (Picador, 2019), by permission of the publisher; Ian Stephen, 'I'll Boil the Kettle', from *Providence II* (The Windfall Press, 1994), by permission of the author; Kenneth Steven, 'Iona Ferry', from *Island: Collected Poems* (St Andrew Press, 2009), by permission of the author; Gerda Stevenson, 'Reconstructed Head of a Young Woman', from *Quines* (Luath Press, 2018), by permission of the author; Sheila Templeton, 'Lighthouses', from *Shorelines* (Federation of Writers (Scotland), 2012), by permission of the author; Ruaraidh MacThòmais/Derick Thomson, 'An Dàrna Eilean/The Second Island', from *Creachadh na Clàrsaich* (Macdonald, 1982), by permission of the publisher; Samuel Tongue, 'Hauling-Out', from *Sacrifice Zones* (Red Squirrel Press, 2020), by permission of the author; Roseanne Watt, 'The Moon Jellyfish', from *Moder Dy* (Polygon, 2019), by permission of the publisher; James Knox Whittet, 'Island Wedding', from *100 Islands Poems of Great Britain and Ireland* (Iron Press, 2005), by permission of the author; Hamish Whyte, 'My Son's Photograph of Shells at Kildonan', from *A Bird in the Hand* (Shoestring Press, 2008), by permission of the author.

Every effort has been made to trace copyright holders of the poems published in this book. The editor and publisher apologise if any material has been included without appropriate acknowledgement, and would be glad to receive any information on poets and their estates we have not been able to trace.

* * *

I am especially grateful to Lizzie Macgregor and Hamish Whyte for their guidance and supportiveness throughout; to Christine De Luca, Tom Pow, Donald Smith and Colin Waters for help and a ready ear; and in the Aladdin's cave of the Scottish Poetry Library to Gillian Hamnett, Emily Prince and latterly Rod Hunt. For the anthology's appearance under the Birlinn/Polygon imprint I particularly acknowledge Hugh Andrew's initial encouragement, the enabling hand of poetry editor Edward Crossan and the role of cover designer Rose Cooper. My thanks to the poets themselves for the pleasure I hope their work will bring. And I am deeply indebted to my wife Judy, my constant sounding-board and an indispensable touchstone for the flavour of the volume as a whole.

SC

INDEX OF POETS